The Essential Guide
to TCP/IP Commands

The Essential Guide to TCP/IP Commands

Martin R. Arick

John Wiley & Sons, Inc.
• New York • Chichester • Brisbane
• Toronto • Singapore

Publisher: Katherine Schowalter
Editor: Robert Elliott
Managing Editor: Susan Curtin
Text Design & Composition: Publishers' Design and Production Services, Inc.

Library of Congress Cataloging-in-Publication Data:

Arick, Martin R.
    The essential guide to TCP/IP commands / Martin R. Arick,
      p. cm.
    Includes index.
    ISBN 0-471-12569-5 (pbk. : alk. paper)
    1. TCP/IP (Computer network protocol) I. Title
  TK5105.585.A75   1996
  004.6'2—dc20   95-41515
                                                   CIP

Printed in the United States of America

10 9 8 7 6 5 4 3 2 1

Contents

List of Figures

Preface

Transmission Control Protocol/Internet Protocol (TCP/IP) provides the services necessary to interconnect processors and to interconnect networks. TCP/IP is the most widely used protocol available today. Nearly every UNIX system supports it and most other non-UNIX systems have software that supports TCP/IP available to them. The wide availability of common networking software has led to the growth of large complex networks that mix various types of computer systems. From a user's point of view, TCP/IP operates at two distinct levels: (1) TCP/IP provides the common set of rules (protocols) to enable computer-to-computer messaging and (2) TCP/IP provides a set of applications (programs) that enable users to interact with remote processors.

This book mirrors the two-level view of TCP/IP by containing two roughly equal parts. The first part describes the use of these protocols to provide a suite of applications enabling a user to interact with remote hosts to perform a variety of distributed functions. The second part begins with a description of a widely accepted model of networks, the Open Systems Interconnection (OSI) model and then describes the various protocols of TCP/IP and how these protocols fit into the model of networking.

The first part of the book (Chapters 1–13) concerns itself with applications that the various services of TCP/IP provide. These applications form the basis for the user to interact with the TCP/IP protocols. This part of the book is user-oriented and focuses on the "how tos" of these applications with practical examples of their use followed by discussion of how the underlying TCP/IP services make these applications work. The first part of each chapter discusses how the user would interact with the application in a simple way to use the service of the application. The second part of the chapter covers more advanced ways of using the application. The problems that the user can have with the application are covered in a section titled "Pitfalls to Avoid." Next, sections follow on how this command would be used (if at all) on personal computers (PCs) and within the Internet. Finally, how the application works is covered in a section titled "Behind the Scenes." Thus, a user can read the first parts of a chapter as a "how-to" document without needing to learn the insides of a particular application.

The first application that is discussed in Chapter 2 is the way users can log in to a remote system and execute commands on that remote system. Chapter 3 focuses on a more general application service that allows users to connect to a particular server on a remote host and use the services of that server. Chapter 4 discusses copying files between two hosts, while Chapter 5 describes how to execute commands on a remote host without logging into that host. The first of two chapters (6 and 7) on file transfer applications describes a simple file transfer method suitable for diskless workstations and terminal servers, and the second chapter describes a fully functional file transfer application that can perform filename services and changing of directories and a host of other filenaming services as well as transferring files. Sending and receiving electronic mail is the subject of Chapter 8. Chapter 9 examines network file services and how remote file systems can be made available locally. Chapter 10 looks at a set of miscellaneous network services such as message echo, pattern printing, and so forth. The Internet and the special commands of the Internet are covered in Chapter 11. An in-depth look at some of the files that form part of the UNIX implementation of TCP/IP follows in Chapter 12. This first section concludes with Chapter 13, an examination of some of the security and performance issues of a network.

The second part of the book concentrates on the user-invisible parts of TCP/IP networks to provide a foundation for understanding how TCP/IP applications work. Chapter 14 examines the ISO model of networks to provide a framework for analyzing and discussing TCP/IP-based networks. Chapter 15 provides an overview of the TCP/IP protocols describing what functions are provided by each of the protocols. The various TCP/IP protocols in the network layer (Internet protocols) are described in Chapters 16 and 17, while Chapter 18 describes the protocols of the transport layer (Transmission Control Protocol).

One note on terminology: The term "internet" is used throughout this book to mean collections of networks and their interconnection, particularly in reference to networking protocols. The term "Internet" refers to the specific collection of networks that are organized by the Internet Architecture Board.

1

A Real-World Internetworking Protocol: TCP/IP

During the middle to late 1960s the first attempts were made to interconnect a number of computers together. By the late 1960s networks containing numbers of processors were formed and operational. A number of far-thinking people began working on being able to connect separate networks together to form a distributing computing system. In this period of time the Department of Defense had a need to interconnect many of its computers in a distributed manner that would survive a nuclear war. The Advanced Research Projects Agency (ARPA) sponsored the effort to create a set of hardware and software to accomplish the interconnectivity of networks, even ones whose internal software was not identical. Thus, ARPANET was born. The interconnectivity in ARPANET required the use of dedicated processors called Interface Messaging Processors (IMPs) and leased point-to-point lines to interconnect them. A primary service offered by ARPANET was resource sharing; thus, a researcher in one network could connect onto a host in another network to use that host which might be a supercomputer.

At the same time that ARPANET was established and growing, several other networking technologies were coming of age such as Ethernet, Token Ring, and so forth. These technologies also used dedicated hardware and software to interconnect hosts. Thus, a new problem arose: how to interconnect two different kinds of networks? Each of the network types uses a particular set of hardware and software to effect interconnectivity within a homogenous network, but these sets of hardware/software are incompatible with each other. What was needed was a set of software that operated on top of the networking methodologies that could manage the information exchange between two different networks.

The problem that the designers of TCP/IP needed to solve is illustrated in Figure 1.1: Host A and Host B desire to exchange information with each other. Whether they are on the same physical network as in Figure 1.2 or on different networks as in Figure 1.3 need not be apparent to either host. In fact, only the name of the host with which to communicate should be needed. From the user's point of view, Host A can be seen as the host the user is on and Host B as a remote host with which the user is trying to communicate. From the user's point of view, hosts and networks look something like Figure 1.4 where the "cloud" represents all the hardware and software that is between the local host that the user is on and the remote host with which the user wants to communicate.

The most desired basic service is one based on moving information from one host to another. Thus, the first part of the problem is software that will be able to move information from one host to another regardless of the networking methodology used.

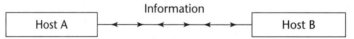

FIGURE 1.1   Model of two communicating hosts.

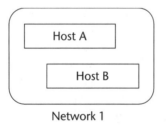

FIGURE 1.2   Two communicating hosts in the same network.

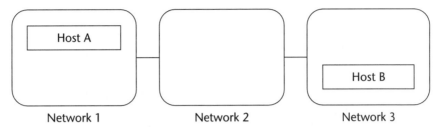

FIGURE 1.3   Two communicating hosts in different networks.

FIGURE 1.4   User's view of networks.

Further, the existence of incompatible networking methodologies must be acknowledged and overcome. The first piece of this software is the Internet Protocol software which sits on top of the networking methodologies and manages the addressing of one host to another and the fragmentation of packets due to networks with differing message sizes. But this protocol does not provide reliable data transport. Applications might want reliable data exchange; this is added via the Transmission Control Protocol (TCP). (For applications that do not need reliable data exchange, User Datagram Protocol (UDP) is available which is much simpler to implement but provides less services.)

To make the problem more approachable the designers came up with several sets of services that could be used by either their own applications or foreign applications. Each of the sets of services that the application could use were called *protocols*, sets of rules that could be used by other applications. This approach led to a natural form of layering by assigning different layers different functions that need to be available for internetworking to function. Figure 1.5 enlarges on the problem Figure 1.1 showed and adds some distinct software layers to the origi-

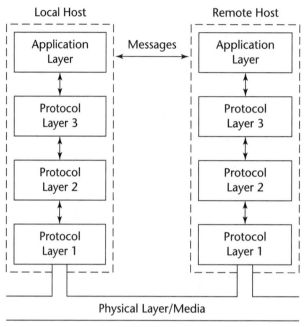

FIGURE 1.5   Layered model of communicating hosts.

nal view as shown in Figure 1.1. In this depiction, the host to which the user is connected is called the *Local Host* and the host with which the user wants to communicate is called the *Remote Host*. This particular model has only four layers, while other models might have more (or less). In this model a message is being sent from the application layer on the local host to the application layer on the remote host.

Returning once more to the layered model shown in Figure 1.5, the names of the protocols that TCP/IP will provide in this model can be added. This group of protocols includes Internet Protocol and Transmission Control Protocol, as discussed in earlier sections. But, in fact, a number of other protocols have been added to solve various problems that internetworking leads to. Figure 1.6 details the major protocols and some of the applications that the TCP/IP suite contains. The TCP/IP applications will be discussed in the first part of this book; then each of these protocols which solves a particular networking problem will be described in some detail in the second half of the book.

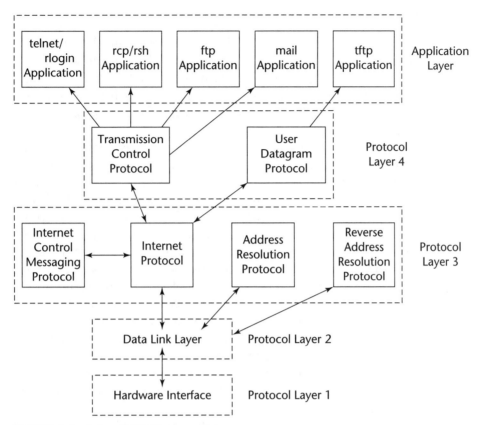

FIGURE 1.6 Suite of TCP/IP protocols.

Early designers determined that three types of services were considered the minimum needed for a fully functioning internetwork:

1. Mail services to exchange messages between hosts
2. File transfer services to move files from one host to another
3. Terminal services to allow connection and execution of commands on a host remote from a terminal

Each of these types of services is part of the TCP/IP software suite and is offered as an application which uses the other elements of the protocol suite itself.

These early developers of TCP/IP quickly recognized that

the only methodology that could accomplish the task of wide availability would be to establish standard procedures for the functions that networks need to perform. They understood that these procedures need not specify how the task was to be accomplished, only how one processor would view its interaction with the network and its interaction with other processors with which it wanted to communicate.

To promulgate these ideas and to encourage software to be written for a variety of processors and operating systems, the sponsors of TCP/IP began to publish a series of documents that would develop the basis for this internetworking methodology (available from several sources, including networks, of course). These documents were published as discussion documents to be commented on: They were named Request for Comments or RFCs for short. The goal of this series of documents was to both inform (provide the basis for an internetworking protocol) and to encourage discussion of features that would be needed for internetworking capabilities. Over the years most of the original documents have been superseded by revised versions and extensions have been added along the way. Some of these documents were just commentary on the process; others were commentary on life. The original series of documents was published in the middle to late 1970s.

Publication of the standards within the TCP/IP suite has led to TCP/IP services being offered on nearly all types of computers from IBM mainframes to personal computers. In addition, many applications have been written which use the TCP/IP protocol suite to accomplish the network functions that they need to use. One such application, Network File Systems (NFS) from Sun Microsystems Corporation, is so widely available that Chapter 9 will examine how it operates. Implementation of TCP/IP services on personal computers has led these units to become full-fledged network hosts, able to perform all of the services outlined in this book.

QUICK GUIDE TO THE COMMANDS OF TCP/IP

The next chapters will focus on the standard applications that have been created to solve specific networking problems of the

Operation	Command	Chapter
Logging into a Remote System	rlogin	3
Connecting to a Remote System	telnet	4
Copying Files from Host to Host	rcp	5
Executing Commands on a Remote Host	rsh	6
Simple File Transfer	tftp	7
Transferring Files between Hosts	ftp	8
Electronic Mail Services	mail	9
Network File Systems	mount	10
Miscellaneous Network Services	telnet	11

FIGURE 1.7   TCP/IP standard applications.

users. These applications use the various parts of the TCP/IP protocol suite to perform their particular function. Figure 1.7 summarizes the applications that are available, showing the command that invokes the particular application.

Logging into a Remote System (rlogin Command)

Users desiring to run commands interactively on a remote host can use the **rlogin** command to establish a connection on the remote host and cause the **login** command to be started in the name of the requesting user. Unless otherwise specified, the requesting user is the user who executed the **rlogin** command on the local host. Once the connection is established, all further keystrokes entered on the local host are passed to the remote host and all output generated on the remote host is displayed on the terminal of the local host. An optional argument can be used to invoke a login session on a remote host in the name of a different user. The **rlogin** command is discussed in detail in Chapter 3.

Connecting to a Remote System (telnet Command)

Users desiring to connect to a remote system and interact with any of the various servers on a remote system can use the **telnet** command. Executing the **telnet** command with just the name of the remote host will cause a login session to begin on the remote host. A variety of **telnet** commands are available to control the connection with the remote host. The **telnet** command models all terminals as Network Virtual Terminals (NVT) which are simplified ASCII devices with keyboards and printers. Support of more advanced terminal functions is negotiated between telnet client and server. Telnet support is available on a wide range of disparate computer systems. The **telnet** command can be used to connect to a particular TCP Port number which may invoke some specialized service such as configuring a terminal server. Users would use **telnet** instead of the **rlogin** command if they wished to exercise more control over the functioning of the connection.

Copying Files from Host to Host (rcp Command)

Copying files from one host to another is most easily accomplished using the **rcp** command. Whole directories can also be copied with one command. Ordinarily the command operates in the name of the user on the local system that invoked it, but optional arguments can be used to specify the names of other users under which to perform the command. Files remote from the local host can be copied from one remote host to another.

Executing Commands on a Remote System (rsh Command)

Commands can be executed on a remote host without logging into it by using the **rsh** command. The output from the command is returned to the local host as if the command was executed on the local host. Any host to which the user has access can have commands executed on it. Normally, the commands are executed on the remote host in the name of the user on the local host that executed the **rsh** command, but an optional argument can be used to identify a different user under which the command on the remote host will be executed.

Simple File Transfer (tftp Command)

Transferring one file from one system to another can be accomplished using the **tftp** command. Only reading or writing files is supported and no validation of the command is performed. No directory operations are performed. **tftp** uses UDP as its transport protocol and, thus, implementation of **tftp** is simplified. **tftp** is suitable for loading diskless workstations and terminal servers.

Transferring Files between Hosts (ftp Command)

Transferring groups of files between hosts is accomplished using the **ftp** command. Moving between both the local and remote directory and listing the contents of directories are supported functions. Multiple selection criteria can be used to select which files to transfer. A command language is available to create scripts of file transfer commands. The **ftp** command can be used to transfer files between dissimilar hosts.

Electronic Mail Services (mail Command)

Properly formatted messages can be sent from one user to another user without the sender knowing where the receiving host is. These messages, usually called *mail messages*, can be sent anywhere in a network by invoking the **mail** command. A complete mail address contains two elements; the name of the user on the remote host and the network address of the remote host. The mail protocol depends on the other protocols to properly route the message to the destination user.

Network File Systems (mount Command)

Files that are physically located on a remote host can be made locally accessible using Network File Systems. Executing a **mount** command can enable a remote file system to appear to be a local file system to a user. Users can treat these network file systems as local file systems. Application programs will not be able to sense whether these file systems are local to the host.

Miscellaneous Network Services

A variety of optional network services are available to use as network test tools or to use to set a standard date and time throughout a network. One service will echo back any characters it is sent to the requesting host while another will send back all of the printable ASCII characters to the requesting host. Two different time services are available: One will return the current date and time while another will return the number of seconds since midnight January 1, 1900.

rlogin Command: Logging into a Remote System

INTRODUCTION

The **rlogin** command is used to log into a remote host and start an interactive terminal session. Once this session is established, all commands that are executed will be executed on the remote host until the session is ended.

This chapter will examine how to use the **rlogin** command, what problems can occur when executing **rlogin** commands, using the **rlogin** command on the personal computer, using the **rlogin** command on the Internet, and how the server that supports the **rlogin** command operates.

GETTING STARTED WITH THE rlogin COMMAND

The syntax for the **rlogin** command is simple, with the name of the remote host you wish to connect to as the only needed option. Thus, the command

```
rlogin goofy
```

will log the local user onto the specified remote host **goofy** and connect the local terminal on which the command was entered to the remote host. The remote host will start a user session in the name of the local user and will request the password for that user on the remote system by replying

```
enter password:
```

to which you would enter the password for your user id on that remote system. Your password on that system can be different from your password on the local system. If the password you entered matched the one known to the remote system, a user session on that remote host would be started. The remote host knows that this particular terminal session was started from a network command, but no particular significance is attached to that knowledge. The **who** command will often display from which remote system the user has connected. The user has the same privileges on the remote host that the user would have if the user was locally attached to the remote host.

The remote terminal type will be the same as the local environment variable TERM. The window size will be the same as the one on the local host, if the remote host supports that particular window size. Ctrl-S and Ctrl-Q key sequences are used to stop and start the flow of information. Input and output buffers will be flushed on interrupts.

The **rlogin** command will run the **login** command on the remote host to start a terminal session under the name of the local user. If a user wants to log in to a remote host under a different name, the -l option is available to specify the name of the user under which you want to execute on the remote host. For example,

```
rlogin goofy -l marty
```

will start an interactive terminal session on the remote host **goofy** under the name *martya*. The interactive session will start in the Home directory of the user (see description of the etc/passwd file in Chapter 12) and the environment will be what the user *martya* has defined.

ADVANCED TIPS AND TECHNIQUES

If an 8-bit path between the local host and the remote host is necessary, the optional parameter -8 can be specified. Thus, the command

```
rlogin goofy -l martya -8
```

will log the user martya onto **goofy** and send and receive 8-bit characters.

The user can interrupt the current login session on the remote host by entering the escape character. By default this escape character is the tilde (~). The escape character will only be recognized as an interrupt if it is the first character on the line, that is, the first character following a carriage return. Entering two escape characters in a row as the first two characters in a line will cause one escape character to be sent to the remote system as an ordinary character. Entering the escape character and a period (.) will cause the connection between the local host and the remote host to be immediately broken.

A different escape character can be specified by using the -e option. For example, the following will change the escape character to a backslash (\ )

```
rlogin goofy -e\
```

during the login session that is started with this command. You would need to specify a different escape character if you want to remotely log into another host from the remote host you are already logged into. If you did not change your escape character and tried to interrupt your **rlogin** session, you would be returned to the original local host.

The **rsh** command when run without further parameters will invoke the **rlogin** command and log in the user on the remote host. You can set up linked files and then just enter the name of the remote host that you want to log into. For example, if you link a file as in

```
ln -s /usr/ucb/rsh goofy
```

and you execute the command

```
goofy
```

a login on **goofy** will be started for the user. The system administrator can create a series of these linked files so that in order to log onto a particular host, the user only needs to type in the name of that host. (A fuller description of how the **rsh** command operates can be found in Chapter 6.) The interactive terminal session on the remote host will continue until the user logs out of the remote host.

If a user wishes to start a session on a remote host under the user name *sam*, and you forget to use the -l option and issue the command

```
rlogin sneezy
```

but want to start the user session under a different user name, you can press the Enter key when prompted for the user's password. The password request will fail and the **rlogin** server on the remote system will then ask for the name of a user with the prompt

```
login:
```

to which you can reply with the name of the user you want to start the session. You will then be prompted for the password for that user.

PITFALLS TO AVOID

The major problem that occurs with the **rlogin** command is that the user on the local system is not known on the remote system. Typically, the message "No such user" will be received. The solution to this problem is either starting the session on the remote host under another name (using the **-l** option) or having the system administrator of the other system add your name to list of valid users.

Another problem that can occur is that the Home directory for the user does not exist. For most UNIX systems, the login attempt will be rejected. The usual cause for a missing Home directory is that it is located on a file server in the network which is currently unavailable. The only solution for this kind of problem is to have the system administrator set up a local Home directory on every system that you wish to use.

Another problem is that for some types of hosts the **rlogin** command may not be supported. For these hosts, the user should try the **telnet** command as that command is more widely implemented.

 ## PC CONSIDERATIONS

The **rlogin** command is widely available for PC systems, both as a DOS application and a Windows application. The DOS version of the **rlogin** command runs from the command line and often has the same set of options that are described earlier in the UNIX implementation of the **rlogin** command, such as specifying a different user name or specifying a different escape character.

In the Windows version of the **rlogin** command, the name and set up of a session with a particular remote host can be defined so that the set up of the session with a particular host can be reused. Even the password can be captured so that when the session with the host is restarted the password will be entered for the user. In addition, some implementations allow the name of the session to be specified as a command line option.

 ## INTERNET CONSIDERATIONS

One of the functions for which the Internet is designed is providing the ability to allow users to connect to remote systems that are not located in their own local network. All of the commands and options discussed earlier in this chapter can be used on the Internet. The one adjustment that must be made has to do with the name of the host to which you wish to connect. If you enter the command

```
rlogin goofy
```

which is a request to start a user session on the host **goofy**, the host that will be found is one in your local network. If, instead, **goofy** was not in your local network but somewhere on the Internet, the address would need to provide more detailed information on where **goofy** was located.

The command

```
rlogin goofy.mycompany.com
```

gives the added information indicating in which network **goofy** is located. Internet addresses are required to be unique so no confusion will exist as to which **goofy.mycompany.com** you wanted to connect to.

As another example, suppose you wanted to start a user session on the host named **master.company.com**. The command you would enter is

```
rlogin master.company.com
```

which will request a user session on **master.company.com**. The host **master.company.com** will request a password (just like your local host would) and, if you enter the correct password, will start the user session. After the user session has started, the interaction with the remote host will proceed just as it would if you were connected to a host in your own local network.

BEHIND THE SCENES

The **rlogin** command sends a message to the **rlogin** server on the remote host. This server is listening at port number 49 for a request to start a user session on this host. The request will be validated by the **rlogin** server before a user session will be started. As shown in Figure 2.1, the TCP protocol is used to ensure that the messages from host to host are sequenced properly.

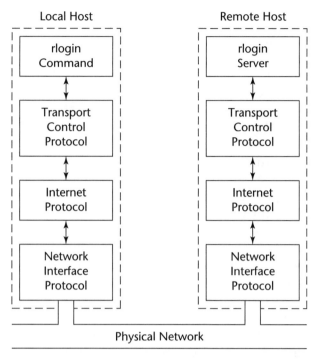

FIGURE 2.1   rlogin interaction with other TCP/IP protocols.

How does the **rlogin** server work? If the request for connection is received by the **rlogin** server, then the validation process is as follows:

1. The source port number is checked to make sure that it is between 512 and 1,023 and is thus, a trusted requester.
2. The **rlogin** server validates the client user:

   rlogin server looks up the local user's name in the /etc/passwd file, then changes to the directory stored there. If either the look-up or the directory change fail, the user is not validated.

   If the user id is not 0 (that is to say, this is not the root user), the /etc/hosts.equiv file is searched for the name of the local host trying to log in. If the name is in the file, the user is validated. If the name of the local host is not present in the file, then the Home directory of the user is checked for a .rhosts file and that file is searched for the name of the local host.

If the user validation fails, the **rlogin** server will prompt the user for the password which will be checked in the /etc/passwd file on the remote host. After the user is validated, the **rlogin** server allocates a pseudo-terminal (called a "pty") and connects standard input, standard output, and standard error to it.

The **rlogin** server propagates the baud rate and terminal type as found in the environment variable TERM. The first message that the server receives from the client contains the baud rate and the terminal type.

The window size is requested by the client and the server will attempt to provide that service. This process is called *negotiation*. Further, if there are changes to the window size during the life of the connection, this too would be requested from the server. The window size is requested by the client by sending a 12-byte message to the server, as detailed in Figure 2.2. By describing the window that is desired, the **rlogin** command is requesting that the **rlogin** server on the remote host provide a similar window.

One issue of security: The **rlogin** command is sometimes used in place of the **telnet** command because system administrators can set up user validation so that no password is needed for a user to log in on another host. The **telnet** command always requires a password to be entered. Unfortunately, this approach, while convenient for users, opens a security hole on the remote system when used.

Byte		1:	Hexadecimal FF
Byte		2:	Hexadecimal FF
Byte		3:	Ascii lowercase "s"
Byte		4:	Ascii lowercase "s"
Bytes	5 and	6:	Number of Character Rows
Bytes	7 and	8:	Number of Characters per Row
Bytes	9 and	10:	Number of Pixels in the x direction
Bytes	11 and	12:	Number of Pixels in the y direction

FIGURE 2.2 Window size request by **rlogin** client.

SUMMARY

A session can be started on a remote host in order to execute commands on the remote host by executing the **rlogin** command. Once the session is established, all commands entered are executed on the remote host until the session is ended by use of the **logout** command. An optional argument can be used to change the user of the session on the remote host.

For further study, look at the manual pages for the **rlogin** command on your particular UNIX host. For more details on the under-the-cover operation of the **rlogin** command, read RFC 1282 entitled "BSD Rlogin" written by B. Kantor in 1991.

telnet Command: Connecting to Remote Hosts

INTRODUCTION

The **telnet** command provides remote login services so that an interactive user on a client system can connect with a server on a remote system. By default, the server is the **telnet** server to provide an interactive terminal session to execute commands on the remote host. But other servers, such as the **mail** server or the **ftp** server, can also be connected to directly. Once a connection is established, the client process on the local host passes the user's keystrokes to whichever server process it was connected. If that server process was the **telnet** server, a login session will be started. The **telnet** command uses TCP as the protocol to ensure error checking.

When the **telnet** command establishes a connection with a remote host, it maps the local terminal into a model of a terminal called a Network Virtual Terminal (NVT) which is described fully later in this chapter. The NVT is an imaginary device which has a printer and a keyboard and can print the full set of 7-bit ASCII characters. Each end of the telnet connection performs the same mapping functions so that neither end of the connection knows (or cares) what kind of terminal is actually being used. Negotiation of the availability of some services will take place with either end of the connection offering a service or requesting a service which needs to be performed by the other end of the connection. This offer can be refused by either end of the connection.

This chapter will examine how to use the **telnet** command, what problems can occur when executing **telnet** commands, using the **telnet** command on the personal computer, using the **telnet** command on the Internet, and how the server that supports the **telnet** command operates.

GETTING STARTED WITH THE telnet COMMAND

The simplest use of the **telnet** command is to establish an interactive terminal session with a remote host to execute commands on that remote host. To do this, enter the following:

```
telnet ranch
```

This will cause the **telnet** command to establish a connection with the remote host named **ranch** and the following will display on your terminal,

```
trying . . . .
Connection to ranch
Escape character is "^T"
```

followed by several blank lines. Then the **telnet** command will start a login session with the host named **ranch**. This remote host will prompt for your login name and then your login password. After both responses have been entered and validated, commands are executed on that remote host from then on until the **logout** command is entered or the telnet session is halted. Entering whatever escape character was specified when you connected to the remote host will return control to the local host. These escape sequences will differ depending on what kind of host you are connected to. Once you enter the escape character, control will be transferred to the local host (while the connection to the remote host is maintained) and the following will be displayed on the local terminal:

```
telnet>
```

On some systems, a different escape character can be specified as an option to the **telnet** command as in

```
telnet -e ^A ranch
```

which will enable Ctrl+A to operate as an escape sequence for this telnet session. On other systems, you need to specify the escape character in the command mode using the **escape** command. You can tell that a different escape character has been defined by examining the messages that you receive from the remote host when the connection has been made. The first or second message should be

```
escape character is "^A"
```

which indicates the escape character has been redefined to be Ctrl+A. You should use a different escape sequence if you are using telnet to log onto one remote system from another remote system that you connected to using a **telnet** command.

Several levels of help and status displays are available. To get a display of information about which commands are available and what they do, enter the following,

```
telnet> help
```

the output of which is illustrated in Figure 3.1; then the telnet prompt will again be displayed.

To find out the current settings of the various special characters, enter

```
telnet> set ?
```

which will display how the various special characters are set up, as shown in Figure 3.2.

Commands may be abbreviated. Commands are:

close	Close current connection
display	Display operating parameters
emulate	Emulate a vt100 or 3270 terminal
mode	Try to enter line-by-line or character-at-a-time
open	Connect to a site
quit	Exit telnet
send	Transmit special characters ('send ?' for more)
set	Set operating parameters ('set ?' for more)
status	Print status information
toggle	Toggle operating parameters ('toggle ?' for more)
z	Suspend telnet
?	Print help information

FIGURE 3.1 Available **telnet** commands.

echo	character to toggle local echoing on/off
escape	character to escape back to telnet command mode
erase	character to cause an erase character
flushoutput	character to cause an abort output
interrupt	character to cause an interrupt process
kill	character to cause an erase line
quit	character to cause a break
eof	character to cause an EOF
sak	character to cause remote host SAK sequence to be sent
?	character to display help information

FIGURE 3.2 telnet special character functions.

If you wanted to display how the various toggled options are currently set, you would enter the command

```
telnet> toggle ?
```

which is illustrated in Figure 3.3.

Another display of operating parameters can be obtained by entering the command

```
telnet> display
```

the output of which is illustrated in Figure 3.4.

If you want to know the current condition of a connection to a remote host, you can execute the **status** command and the response would be

```
Connected to hosta.company.com.
Operating in character-at-a-time mode.
Escape character is '^T'.
```

which indicates that a connection has been made to the remote host **hosta.company.com** and you are operating in the character-at-a-time mode.

Another level of help is available by using the command

```
telnet> send ?
```

which is illustrated in Figure 3.5.

autoflush	toggle flushing of output when sending interrupt characters
autosynch	toggle automatic sending of interrupt characters in urgent mode
crmod	toggle mapping of received carriage returns
localchars	toggle local recognition of certain control characters
debug	toggle debugging output
netdata	toggle printing of hexadecimal network data for debugging
options	toggle viewing of options processing for debugging

FIGURE 3.3   telnet toggle options.

will flush output when sending interrupt characters.

won't send interrupt characters in urgent mode.

won't map carriage return on output.

won't recognize certain control characters.

won't turn on socket level debugging.

won't print hexadecimal representation of network traffic.

won't show option processing.

[^E]	echo.
[^T]	escape.
[^H]	erase.
[^O]	flushoutput.
[^C]	interrupt.
[^U]	kill.
[^\]	quit.
[^D]	eof.
[off]	sak.

Not emulating (native type vt220)

FIGURE 3.4   Display of current telnet operating parameters.

Send Option	*What Option Does*
ao	Send Telnet Abort output
ayt	Send Telnet 'Are You There'
brk	Send Telnet Break
ec	Send Telnet Erase Character
el	Send Telnet Erase Line
escape	Send current escape character
ga	Send Telnet 'Go Ahead' sequence
ip	Send Telnet Interrupt Process
nop	Send Telnet 'No operation'
sak	Send Telnet Secure Attention Key
synch	Perform Telnet 'Synch operation'

FIGURE 3.5   Available telnet send options.

For example, if you execute the **send ayt** while connected to a VMS system, you will get the response

```
RANCH::COWBOY 23:06:10 (DCL) CPU=00:00:01.02
PF=537 IO=98 MEM=265
```

which indicates you are connected to a VMS system called **RANCH**.

Entering the **telnet** command by itself on the command line

```
telnet
```

will start the telnet process and the prompt

```
telnet>
```

will appear on your terminal. You are now in command mode and can connect to any host. You can also set up the various modes of the **telnet** command as discussed in a later part of this chapter. In the command mode, you can start a login session with a remote host named **chippy** by entering the command

```
open chippy
```

which will begin an interactive login session with the remote host.

 ADVANCED TIPS AND TECHNIQUES

When using the **telnet** command, you may choose an 8-bit input and output path using two different command line options as in

```
telnet -8 -L ranch
```

You can combine these various command line options. Thus, the command

```
telnet -e ^B -8 ranch
```

will cause a connection to be made to the remote host named **ranch** using an 8-bit pathway Ctrl+B as the escape character.

If you wanted to connect to the remote mail server on a remote host you would enter the **telnet** command followed by the *well-known* port number of the mail server which is 25. These well-known port numbers can be found in the /etc/services file (see Chapter 12 entitled "A Guide to TCP/IP Files" for further details). For example, the command

```
telnet rover 25
```

will cause the following output on your terminal

```
Trying...
Connected to rover.
Escape character is "^]".
220 rover Sendmail AIX 3.x/xxx xxx/xxx ready at xxx
```

indicating that you are connected to the mail server on **rover**. You would now enter the commands that the mail server would use. (One way to find out the commands that the server recognizes is to enter the character "?"; usually, the server will list the commands that it knows about.)

As another example, suppose you wanted to connect to the **ftp** server directly and not use the **ftp** command (see Chapter 7 for more information on the **ftp** command). The well-known port number for the **ftp** server is 21. If you enter the command

```
telnet rover 21
```

it will cause the following output on your terminal

```
Trying...
Connected to rover.
Escape character is "^]".
220 rover FTP server (Version xxx Date xxxxx) ready.
```

indicating that you are connected to the **ftp** server on **rover**. You would now enter the commands that the mail server would use.

Another method of connecting to various servers via the **telnet** command is to enter the **telnet** command by itself as in

```
telnet
```

which will start the **telnet** command; you will get the following prompt on your terminal:

```
telnet>
```

You can now use the **open** command with the name of the host and port number that you want to connect with on the remote host as in the command

```
open rover 21
```

which will connect to the **ftp** server on **rover**.

Another way to use the **telnet** command is to connect to network devices and configure them. Often these network devices have a special port number set aside for the system console; usually the port number is 2048. For these devices the following will connect to them to configure them

```
telnet termserver 2048
```

which will cause a connection to be made to the device called *termserver* using port number 2048. The network device will often start the network connection by requesting a user name and may even require a password. Once connected, any commands that you enter will be executed by the program controlling the network device. The content of these commands is determined by the network device itself and differs from network device to network device. This type of **telnet** connection can enable you to configure your network devices, such as terminal servers, from one central location.

Once connected to a remote host, you can change from character-at-a-time to line-at-a-time or change whether you are sending carriage return/line feed or just line feed by issuing the **telnet** command. You can also change the special characters that invoke the **telnet** commands (see Figure 3.7). The **telnet** command will attempt to negotiate with the remote host what local terminal type to be on the remote host. Terminal negotiation is not supported by all telnet hosts. Telnet will attempt to emulate a VT100 terminal. Telnet will also emulate a 3270 terminal if either end of the telnet connection is an IBM computer. Terminal negotiation can be disabled on the requesting hosts. Usually there is an environment variable that will control what characters constitute the alternate telnet escape character other than the default Ctrl-T.

The **telnet** command can be used to connect from a UNIX system to a remote system that is running VMS because both ends of the connection can emulate a VT100 type of terminal. When a login connection is requested on a remote host, the **telnet** command will negotiate with the **telnet** server on the remote host which terminal type to emulate. This emulation functionality shields any differences in the underlying operating system or hardware which might affect character representations or character ordering in messages from the user. These services would be found in the OSI model in layer 6, the presentation layer. The **telnet** command can provide these terminal services to the user.

While in the command mode, the command

```
mode line
```

will set the input mode to line-by-line while

```
mode character
```

will set the input mode to character-at-a-time.
While in the command mode

```
open Host [Port]
```

will open a connection to the specific host at the specific port if specified. If no port is given, the **telnet** server will be connected to the **telnet** server on the remote host which will start a login session on that remote host.

To control whether input should be echoed to the local terminal, the variable echo can be set on or off to set the local echo on or off. To close a connection with a remote host, enter the command: **close**. To get a list of commands, enter the character: **?**. To end a telnet session, enter the command: **quit**. To get a snapshot of the current status of the connection with a remote host, enter the command: **status**. To get a list of the settings of the various modes of the **telnet** command, enter the command: **display**. All of these commands must be issued in command mode, not in input mode. You can switch from input mode to command mode by entering the command: **Ctrl-T**; that is to say, you press both the Ctrl key and the T key at the same time. (This pair of keys can be changed. See later instructions.) You can control how telnet responds to a variety of local and remote events by toggling one of the following parameters.

You would toggle "crmod" to map carriage returns sent by the remote hosts to both a carriage return and a line feed. Use this when the host you are dealing with does not send a line feed with its carriage returns.

You can also control what special characters are used to send control sequences to the remote host for operations such as synchronizing output, interrupting the process on the remote host, and so forth. These special characters are translated by the **telnet** command into special commands that the telnet client process sends to the **telnet** server on the remote host to request services such as erasing characters, flushing output, and so forth. These special services can be requested directly through the telnet command mode by entering "send xxxxxx" and the correct argument to the service needed. Multiple arguments can be included on the same request separated by blanks. Figure 3.6 lists the argument that you add to the **send** command that you can use to effect the various services that are needed. Some services have special character sequences associated with them; they are listed in Figure 3.7.

As an example, to interrupt the process on the remote system, you would go into command mode and enter the command **send ip**. You could also enter the local terminal's interrupt character. Such a request can be made at any time but is usually

Service Required	Send Argument
Abort Output	ao
Break or Kill	brk
Erase Character	ec
Erase Line	el
Send Escape Code	escape
Interrupt Process	ip
Are You There	ayt
Go Ahead	ga
No Operation	nop
Secure Attention Key	sak
Synchronize	synch

FIGURE 3.6 telnet send command arguments.

Service Required	Special Character	Default Special Character
Abort Output	flushoutput	Ctrl-O
Break or Kill	quit	Local Terminal Quit Character
Erase Character	erase	Local Terminal Erase Character
Erase Line	kill	Local Terminal Erase Character
Send Escape Code	escape	Ctrl-T
Interrupt Process	interrupt	Local Terminal Interrupt Character

FIGURE 3.7 telnet special character commands.

sent because no response from the remote host has been received recently.

Several entries in Figures 3.6 and 3.7 require explanation. The send argument "ayt" sends a request to the **telnet** server asking it to respond. Such a request can be made at any time, but is usually sent because no response from the remote system has been received recently.

The send argument "ga" tells the **telnet** server to return control to the local user because all the output has been sent to the remote terminal. You should perform the line turn around function since the line is now available to be turned around for transmission from the other end. This is especially valuable for half-duplex lines.

The send argument "synch" causes the remote server to discard all previously typed input that has not been read and processed without dropping the connection. The send argument "sak" causes the remote server to invoke a *trusted shell* if it supports that mode. Normally, when telnet connects to another system, the **login** command is started with the requesting user as a nonprivileged user. If you need privileges, you can request them this way. If the remote system does not support this, the message, "Remote side does not support SAK" will be returned.

The operation of these special characters can be controlled by the setting of a variable, localchars. When it is set "off," the special characters (such as ctrl, etc.) are sent through to the remote host as literal characters. When localchars is set "on," these special character sequences are recognized as requesting services of the **telnet** server.

For more examples of the use of the **telnet** command, examine Chapter 11 where each of a set of network services is invoked by using the **telnet** command with a special port number.

 PITFALLS TO AVOID

The main problem that the **telnet** command has is that the remote system to which the user wishes to connect does not have that user's id registered. If you are known on the remote system by another name, you can use that name as part of the **telnet** command as illustrated earlier in the chapter.

Since the terminal that the **telnet** command requires is so simple, there are few problems with local terminals sending strange control codes. The **telnet** command will ignore whatever unusual codes it receives and will continue the connection.

PC CONSIDERATIONS

Since the type of terminal that needs to be emulated for the **telnet** command is a simple one, many PC implementations of the **telnet** command have been created. For the DOS version of the **telnet** command, the command is entered just as shown earlier in the chapter with the name of the remote host to connect to being specified as a command-line argument. Once the initial connection is made, the login sequence is much the same with the user id being asked for first, followed by the password for that user id.

For the Windows version of the **telnet** command, the parameters for a particular session can be defined, such as the name of the remote host, the name of the user id that is valid on that host, and even the password to send to that host when requested. Often these parameters can be stored in a named file and recalled when a connection to a particular host is desired.

INTERNET CONSIDERATIONS

The Internet provides the ability to log into a remote computer that is at another site on the Internet using the **telnet** command. That computer can be anywhere in the Internet. The syntax for the **telnet** command would be modified so that the Internet name of the remote host would be specified. Thus, the command might look like

```
telnet jack.company.com
```

which will cause a connection to the remote host **jack.company. com** to be made. After the connection is made, the command is in input mode and all input is sent to the remote host to be processed there.

This type of connection through the Internet network requires only that the user have an account on the remote host, but not on any of the intermediate hosts that are carrying messages between you and the remote computer. The **telnet** command operates just the same whether the computer you are communicating with is in the next room or across the country. Chapter 4 describes the **telnet** command in some detail.

Systems that can be accessed through the Internet provide a range of services, from libraries that place their catalogs online such as the Library of Congress (**locis.loc.gov**) to financial services such as Dow Jones News Service. Some of these systems charge for their services. When you access one of these systems, you enter a user name and password so that the charges for online time can be billed to you. In this case, the command

```
telnet locis.loc.gov
```

will cause a connection to the remote host **locis.loc.gov** to be made. After the connection is made, the command is in input mode and all input is sent to the remote host to be processed there. For this connection, a menu of options will be shown which would allow you to access the Library of Congress catalogue. For other **telnet** connections, a menu of options can be shown once you have logged into the remote host.

BEHIND THE SCENES

The **telnet** command uses the TCP and IP protocols to establish communication with the remote server as illustrated in Figure 3.8. The **telnet** server listens at its assigned port number (23) until a request is received. When a request for a service is received, it performs negotiation of terminal characteristics and then starts a login session on the remote host. The process of negotiation requires exchange of a series of telnet messages until both ends of the telnet connection have agreed on services provided.

Telnet commands consist of at least a 2-byte sequence, the first byte of which is the command escape character (IAC) followed by the code that indicates what command is requested. All of the send functions shown in Figure 3.6 and the special character operations shown in Figure 3.7 are implemented using this form of **telnet** command. Figure 3.9 shows what code value is used for each of the requested functions in Figures 3.6 and 3.7.

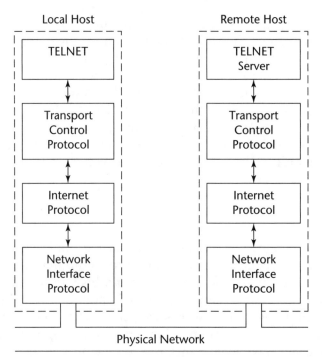

FIGURE 3.8 telnet interaction with other TCP/IP protocols.

Name	Code	What Code Does
NOP	241	No operation
Data Mark	242	The data stream portion of a Synch. This should always be accompanied by a TCP Urgent notification.
Break	243	NVT character BRK
Interrupt Process	244	The function IP
Abort output	245	The function AO
Are You There	246	The function AYT
Erase character	247	The function EC
Erase Line	248	The function EL
Go ahead	249	The GA signal
IAC	255	Data Byte 255

FIGURE 3.9 Decimal code values for special telnet functions.

In addition, telnet commands are used to manage the negotiation process. Figure 3.10 lists the various negotiation commands and what they mean. The WILL, WON'T, DO, DON'T
methodology requires that one party to the telnet connection
can send a WILL XXX command to indicate that he, she, or it
will begin to perform a particular option XXX. DO XXX and
DON'T XXX indicate the other party's acceptance or rejection of
that offer of service. DO XXX is a request that the other party
perform service XXX on the local system and WILL XXX and
WON'T XXX indicate agreement or not to provide that service.
The network virtual terminal is the minimal set of services that
telnet provides and the WILL, WON'T, DO, and DON'T
sequence provides the abilities of both parties to agree on other
mutually beneficial services to provide. It can be expected that
at initial connection time, there will be a flurry of negotiation
requests as each party requests additional services from the
other. Once the negotiation process is complete, few negotiation
requests will occur, but they can if either party wishes. Thus, if

Name	Code	What Code Does
SE	240	End of subnegotiation parameters.
SB	250	Indicates that what follows is subnegotiation of the indicated option.
WILL (option code)	251	Indicates the desire to begin performing, or confirmation that you are now performing, the indicated option.
WON'T (option code)	252	Indicates the refusal to perform, or continue performing, the indicated option.
DO (option code)	253	Indicates the request that the other party perform, or confirmation that you are expecting the other party to perform, the indicated option.
DON'T (option code)	254	Indicates the demand that the other party stop performing, or confirmation that you are no longer expecting the other party to perform, the indicated option.

FIGURE 3.10   Decimal code values for telnet negotiation commands.

a host implements a minimum set of telnet services, it can reject requests for other services without even understanding what services have been asked for.

Negotiation rules include provisions that one party can even add a service temporarily if it wishes to and the other party agrees. Thus, for throughput reasons, it might be advantageous to offer some other services. In addition, negotiation rules require that one party can only request a change in status, but not announce what status it is in. If an option is already on, the request is ignored.

NETWORK VIRTUAL TERMINAL

The Network Virtual Terminal (NVT) is an imaginary device which is used as a model for real terminals but which has a limited set of functions and a specified way of representing data. Telnet hosts will emulate an NVT in conversing with each other. Thus, the real terminal at which a telnet session has begun with its varied data representations will not be visible to the other end of a telnet connection. The translation of data to the format of the NVT is handled by the telnet process. A minimal set of functions is specified for the NVT so that even fairly modest terminals should be supportable. The two telnet partners can negotiate to add services to the minimal set the NVT has. If both partners can agree, some functions can be added.

The NVT is a bidirectional character-based device with a printer and a keyboard. Incoming data is sent to the printer and outgoing data comes from the keyboard. Echoing commands mean echoing the command locally, since it would not be wise to send echoes through the network. The code set supported is 7-bit ASCII characters transmitted in 8-bit bytes. The NVT appears to be half-duplex even though telnet sessions are inherently full-duplex. This choice was made to keep the cost of managing data through a telnet session to a minimum, requiring few data buffers. After the process has finished sending data to the printer and has no queued input from the NVT keyboard, the process must issue the telnet **Go Ahead (GA)** command to turn the line around. This requirement is due to the way the initial terminal (an IBM 2741 terminal) operated: It locked its keyboard after sending its output and waited for its keyboard to be unlocked before allowing more input.

The code set for the NVT includes representations of all 95 ASCII graphics including uppercase and lowercase characters, numbers, punctuation, and so forth. Of the 33 ASCII control codes less than 127 cause the NVT printer to perform some special function. Figure 3.11 lists these control codes. As shown earlier in Figures 3.9 and 3.10, a number of codes above 128 have special meanings.

Character Name	Code	Meaning
Null (NUL)	0	No operation.
Line Feed (LF)	10	Moves the printer to the next print line, keeping the same horizontal position.
Carriage Return (CR)	13	Moves the printer to the left margin of the current line.
Bell (BEL)	7	Produces an audible or visible signal (which does not move the print head).
Back Space (BS)	8	Moves the print head one character position towards the left margin.
Horizontal Tab (HT)	9	Moves the printer to the next horizontal tab stop. It remains unspecified how either party determines or establishes where such tab stops are located.
Vertical Tab (VT)	11	Moves the printer to the next vertical tab stop. It remains unspecified how either party determines or establishes where such tab stops are located.
Form Feed (FF)	12	Moves the printer to the top of the next page, keeping the same horizontal position.

Note: All remaining codes do not cause the NVT printer to take any action.

FIGURE 3.11 Special codes for the NVT printer.

SUMMARY

Establishing a session on a remote host (even a dissimilar one) to interactively execute commands can be performed by executing the **telnet** command. Dissimilar systems can be connected to because telnet uses a model of an ASCII terminal (called the Network Virtual Terminal) and all data is transmitted as if from such a terminal. telnet commands can be used to connect to any of the TCP/IP servers on remote hosts.

Manual pages that describe how the **telnet** command operates form the basis for the operational examples that illustrate how users use telnet. Much of the theoretical discussion in this chapter is based on the RFC that describes the telnet process: J. Postel and J. Reynolds, telnet PROTOCOL SPECIFICATION, RFC 854 (1981). A set of RFCs that describe in detail how many of the individual telnet functions operate are listed in Table A.4 in Appendix A.

rcp Command: Copying Files from Host to Host

INTRODUCTION

The **Remote Copy** (**rcp**) command is used to copy a file (or files) from one host (source) to another host (destination). Either of these hosts may be local to the host from which the command is executed. In addition, the **rcp** command can be used to copy directory trees from one host to another. For flexibility, you can specify the names of users on either host.

This chapter will examine how to use the **rcp** command, what problems can occur when executing **rcp** commands, and how the server that supports the **rcp** command operates.

GETTING STARTED WITH THE rcp COMMAND

In order to perform the simplest of **rcp** commands—to copy a file from one host to another—you would use the syntax

```
rcp helloworld.c ranch:
```

which will copy the contents of helloworld.c that is on the local host to the remote host **ranch** and call it helloworld.c on the remote host. In order to copy a file from one host to another and change its name, you would use the syntax

```
rcp helloworld.c ranch:newworld.c
```

which will copy the contents of helloworld.c that is on the local host to the remote host **ranch** and call it newworld.c. If, alternatively, helloworld.c is on a remote host (**ranch**) and you wish to copy it to your local host and call it newworld.c, you would use:

```
rcp ranch:helloworld.c newworld.c
```

If the name of the file on the local host will be the same as the name of the file on the remote host, the specification of the name on the local host can be replaced with a period (.). Thus,

```
rcp ranch:helloworld.c .
```

will copy helloworld.c from the remote host **ranch** to the local host as helloworld.c. If the file you want to copy is not on the local host but on a remote host (**ranch**) and you want to copy it to a remote host (**sneezy**), you would use

```
rcp ranch:helloworld.c sneezy:newworld.c
```

which would copy helloworld.c on **ranch** to newworld.c on **sneezy**.

If the name of a directory is used as the destination instead of the name of a file, then the source file is copied into the destination directory and keeps its original name. Thus,

```
rcp helloworld.c sneezy:sourcedir
```

indicates that helloworld.c will be copied to sourcedir on **sneezy**. Also, it is possible to list several files that are to be copied into the directory. For example,

```
rcp helloworld.c newworld.c helloworld.h sneezy:sourcedir
```

will cause helloworld.c, newworld.c, and helloworld.h to all be copied into sourcedir on host **sneezy**. If the path of the destination file or directory is not fully qualified (that is to say, does not begin with a /), the path is interpreted as beginning at the Home directory of the remote user account which will be the same as the local user account unless otherwise specified.

If you want to copy a file from a particular directory, you can specify that directory in the **rcp** command. For example, suppose you wanted to get a copy of the hosts file from the host **rodeo**, you would use a command like

```
rcp rodeo:/etc/hosts .
```

which would cause the **rcp** command to examine the /etc directory to find the hosts file in which you are interested. If you had instead entered the command

```
rcp rodeo:etc/hosts .
```

the **rcp** command would have examined the etc directory in your Home directory on the remote host to find the hosts file. In this manner, you could keep copies of system files in their expected subdirectories but in your own Home directory. If you updated the hosts file and wanted to put the file back for the system to use, you would use the command

```
rcp hosts rodeo:/etc/hosts
```

to store that file in your Home directory and the command

```
rcp etc/hosts rodeo:/etc/hosts
```

to keep that file in the etc subdirectory in your Home directory. This latter command would fail if you do not have the privilege to write the /etc/hosts file.

If you maintain just one copy of your .profile startup file (if you use Korn shell) or your .cshrc file (if you use C shell), you can use a script containing **rcp** commands to update all of the hosts on which you have accounts. You would edit your master copy of the .cshrc file and then propagate that file to all of the hosts in your network. Such a script would contain commands like

```
rcp .cshrc rodeo:
rcp .cshrc cowboy:
rcp .cshrc ranch:
```

and so on until you have copied the .cshrc file to all of the remote hosts that you use regularly.

ADVANCED TIPS AND TECHNIQUES

In all of the earlier cases the user name from the local host is used on both the local host and on the remote host. However, it is possible to override that assumption by specifying the name of the user on either the local host or on the remote host by using

```
rcp helloworld.c marty@ranch:newworld.c
```

which would copy helloworld.c (under the local user's name) to helloworld.c on **ranch** under the name of the user *marty*. On the remote host *marty* must have created a file to grant permission to another user to access *marty*'s files. This file (.rhosts file) is described in detail in Chapter 12. Some implementations of this command require a slightly different format for this command. On those systems, the previous command would be specified

```
rcp helloworld.c marty.ranch:newworld.c
```

which would copy helloworld.c onto **ranch** and call it new-world.c.

If you are copying files from one remote host to another, you can specify two different user names if you wish as in

```
rcp marty@ranch:helloworld.c judy@sneezy:newworld.c
```

which would copy helloworld.c on **ranch** as *marty'* to new-world.c to **sneezy** as *judy*. Here again, some UNIX implementa-

tions have a different syntax and this previous command would
then be

```
rcp marty.ranch:helloworld.c judy.sneezy:newworld.c
```

If the destination file exists, its permissions and ownership
will be preserved. If the destination file does not exist, the file
permissions and ownership will be the same as the source file. If
you wish to preserve the modification time of a file, use a special
option (-p) when you perform the **rcp** command.

One last function that the **rcp** command can perform is to
copy an entire directory tree (with all of the files in it) from one
host to another by specifying the names of the source directory
and destination directory as in

```
rcp ranch:sourcedir sneezy:sourcedir
```

which will copy the contents of the sourcedir on **ranch** to
sourcedir on **sneezy**. If the specification of either **ranch** or
sneezy or both is left out, the operation will work the same,
with the local host being used as the source or destination. If
there are subdirectories in the source directory, it will not be
copied unless you add the -r (recursive) flag to your **rcp** command. Thus, the following will copy all of the files and all of the
subdirectories in sourcedir to sourcedir on **sneezy**:

```
rcp -r sourcedir sneezy:sourcedir
```

For both the source directory and destination directory, the user
can be specified. If the name of either or both of the directories
are not fully qualified, the Home directory of the user is added.
Specifying the user to operate as on a remote node, means specifying a different Home directory.

If metacharacters such as *, $, and so forth, are included
in the filename or the directory name, and these need to be
interpreted on the remote host and not on the local host, they
must be enclosed in double quotes (" "), single quotes (' '), or
preceded by a backslash (/) so that the local shell will not interpret them.

PITFALLS TO AVOID

Most of the problems that commonly occur while using the **rcp** command are due to the nonexistence of either the file to be copied, the directory to be copied to or from, or the name of the host. When copying from one host to another, the following are some of the error messages that can occur:

```
host: name ------- not found or --------: host not found
```

Means that the specified host name is not known to the local host. Usually this is due to the absence of the remote host's name in the /etc/hosts file.

```
rcp: -------: not a plain file
```

Means that the form of the **rcp** command that was used required the name of a file and the entry given was not a file (but was probably a directory instead).

```
rcp: invalid user name ------ or rcp: ------- does not
    have an account on this machine
```

Indicates that the user name that you are using on the remote host is not known on that remote host.

```
Permission denied.
```

Indicates that one of the tests that the **rshd** performed failed. Often the message starts with *rsh server:* and indicates that either the user does not exist or does not have access privileges to the user's directory.

PC CONSIDERATIONS

Most TCP/IP implementations for PC do not contain a version of the **rcp** command. Copying files from the local host to the remote host can be accomplished with another command such as **ftp**, so the need to implement a special command to copy from a remote host to a local one is not very pressing.

INTERNET CONSIDERATIONS

Internet hosts do not support **rcp** operations, just as they don't support **rsh** operations. The **ftp** command is available to copy files from one host to another.

BEHIND THE SCENES

Both the **rcp** and the **rsh** commands are serviced by the **rshd** server (or daemon). This server provides for the remote execution of shell commands for the **rsh** command or the execution of the copy command for the **rcp** command. The server operates by listening at the socket number defined in the /etc/services file; usually, the port number is 530. Requests for service arrive at that port from remote hosts (clients) as shown in Figure 4.1.

When a request for service arrives, the server must validate that the request comes from an appropriate client on an appropriate host and is properly formulated. There are several steps that the server follows to ensure this is a proper request.

1. The server checks the source port number of the client that made the request. If the port number is not in the range 0 to 1023, that is to say, one of the port numbers reserved for system functions, the request is denied.
2. The server then reads characters from the socket up to a null byte and uses that number as the port number of a secondary port to use for standard error output. The server

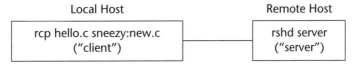

FIGURE 4.1 **rcp** command and its **rshd** server process.

then establishes a second connection with the client's host using the port number it has just read.

3. The server then reads from the socket the name of the user on the client host, the name of the user on the server host, and the command to be executed. The name of the user on the local server is validated in the /etc/passwd file and the Home directory of the user is determined. The current working directory is changed to the Home directory of the user. If either the look-up of the user's name or the change to the user's Home directory fails, the service request is discarded.

4. The name of the client host is looked up in the /etc/hosts.equiv file; if it doesn't exist, the request will be discarded.

5. If the .rhosts file exists in the Home directory of the user, the requesting user is looked up in that file. If this fails, the request is denied.

Once all of these validations have been performed, the command is then passed to the user's login shell. The command(s) is then processed and the interaction between the requesting process and the **rshd** server proceeds as illustrated in Figure 4.2. As indicated in this outline of the steps in the **rcp** process, the error messages can be processed and returned to the requesting process without disrupting the copy process because a second connection is established with the client.

The **rcp** command uses the user name entered for the remote host to determine file access privileges at the remote host. But before that can happen, the **rcp** command determines if it has access to the remote host by determining that the name of the local host is in the remote host's /etc/hosts.equiv file.

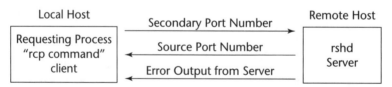

FIGURE 4.2 Establishing connection between **rcp** command and **rshd** server.

The second level of validation is that the user under which the remote copy operation is being done is defined on the remote host. The **rcp** command will permit the copy operation even if the remote user has no password. (Some remote operations require that the user have a password or the operation will be invalidated.)

The third level is to check whether access to the remote user's directories are permitted by examining the .rhosts file in the home directory of the remote user. This file needs to contain entries that specify the remote host and user name. Only those users on those hosts will be able to remotely access this directory. If the .rhosts file does not exist, the copy command will fail if the user does not have access to the remote user's directories. If the user name is specified for the remote host, that user's name is used to set ownership and determine file access privileges that the **rcp** command will use at that host.

SUMMARY

The copying of files from one host to another can be most easily accomplished using the **rcp** command. Manual pages that are found on most UNIX systems form the basis for the discussion of the various options available with the **rcp** command.

5

rsh Command: Executing Commands on Remote Host

INTRODUCTION

The **rsh** command is used to execute a single command on a remote host without logging into that system. Any command for which the user has authority can be executed on a remote host. The output from such a command (if there is any) will be returned to the local host as if the command had been executed on the local host. If no command is specified, the user is logged into the remote host.

This chapter will examine how to use the **rsh** command, what problems can occur when executing **rsh** commands, and how the server that supports the **rsh** command operates.

GETTING STARTED WITH THE rsh COMMAND

Sometimes running just *one* command on a remote host is all that is needed. For example, checking whether a user is defined on a remote host can be done with a single command that is executed on the remote host. Or, as another example, suppose a user wanted to determine what time a remote host believes it to be. Checking the time on another host doesn't require a user to log in; it requires that a single command be executed on the remote host itself and the output of the command be returned to the originating host. As another example, the current processing load on a remote host could be checked. If it is low, users might choose to execute their operations on that host, rather than on the one to which they are locally attached.

Chapters 2 and 3 described how to establish a session on a remote host in order to execute commands on that host. This process of *logging in* requires executing a command which does not return any information to the user but only establishes a connection so that future commands can be executed on the remote host. But in many cases, the information that the user desires or the operation that the user wants to execute are one-step operations. In these cases the logging in operation is wasted; therefore, executing individual commands without logging in may be more efficient for users.

To run single commands on a remote host, the syntax for the **rsh** command is

```
rsh sneezy date
```

This will execute the command **date** on the remote host **sneezy**. As another example, the command

```
rsh sneezy df
```

will request the amount of available free disk space on remote host **sneezy**.

Almost any command can be executed on the remote host. The **rsh** server executes the requested command under the user id of the user on the local host who requested the command. The commands are executed on the remote host using the Home directory of the user (as defined in the /etc/passwd file on the remote host). Thus, files which do not have an absolute path specified for them will be searched for in the Home directory of the user on the remote host. For example,

```
rsh sneezy cp test.c test.bak
```

will look for test.c in the Home directory of the user on the remote host and will copy its contents to test.bak in the Home directory on the remote host **sneezy**.

To execute a command under a different user name, use the -i option on the command line following the name of the remote host. The following command will execute the **cat /etc/passwd** command under the user id *tom*:

```
rsh sneezy -i tom cat /etc/passwd
```

A different user id might be needed if the local user does not have the necessary level of privilege on the remote host or is not even known on the remote host. You will be prompted for the password of the new user that you specified.

Suppose you are looking for a host on which to compile some programs. You probably want to pick one that has the lowest load. You could determine that by using the **rsh** command to query each of the hosts of interest. The command

```
rsh sneezy vmstat
```

might return

```
prcs   memory              page                    faults        cpu
----  ----------   ----------------------  ------------  -----------
 r b   avm  fre re  pi  po  fr  sr  cy  in   sy  cs us sy id wa
 0 0 14877 5376  0   0   0   2  11   0 164  283  95  4  5 88  2
```

as output indicating that this processor is 88 percent idle and a good candidate on which to do some compiling.

As another example, you can check to see if a particular user is defined on a remote host with the command

```
rsh grumpy grep snowwhite /etc/passwd
```

which would return output that looks like

```
snowwhite:x:432:300:Snow White:/u/snoww:/bin/sh
```

to indicate that *snowwhite* is a defined user on that remote system. You would not get any data back that contained the name of the user if that user was not defined on that system.

Output generated by the **rsh** command can be stored in a local file since the output is returned to the local host. The command

```
rsh curley cat source/helloworld.c
```

will display on your terminal the contents of the file source/helloworld.c that is stored on the remote host **curley**. If the source file contains many lines, you might want to use the command

```
rsh curley cat source/helloworld.c | more
```

which will display the file on your terminal one page at a time.

Suppose you wanted to execute a script in the background on another processor while you do some other activities on the local one. The command to start the script looks like

```
rsh sneezy make_donuts
```

which will execute the command **make_donuts** on **sneezy** and return the output to your local system. Now suppose you want to run that same command in the background so that you could do other activities on the local system. If the output cannot be displayed because the **rsh** command is being executed in the background, the **rsh** command will be suspended. Thus, in the following command, output has been redirected to a file

```
rsh sneezy make_donuts > maked.out &
```

You would find that the command is not actually running if you checked its status. Instead you would find

```
[1] + Suspended (tty input) make_donuts > maked.out
```

indicating that the task is waiting for input from you. If the command is to be executed in the background, a special flag (-n) can be used to cause any input to be from the *bit bucket* /dev/null; otherwise the command will halt when the first input is generated. Thus, if you add the -n option and the command was

```
rsh sneezy -n make_donuts > maked.out &
```

you would find that the task is running on the remote host **sneezy**.

 ADVANCED TIPS AND TECHNIQUES

The local shell command will parse any **rsh** command you enter and attempt to interpret any metacharacters that are specified in that command. Suppose you entered the command

```
rsh sneezy cat source/hello.c >> source/bighello.c
```

which will append the contents of source/hello.c from the remote host to the current contents of source/bighello.c on the local host if it exists and if it does not, will create source/bighello.c and fill it with the contents of source/hello.c. The output of the **cat** command ends up on the local host because the shell command on the local host will interpret the >> as a request for the local host to execute. If appending the contents of one remote file to the current contents of another remote file is desired, then the redirection operation >> will need to be shielded from the local shell by using quotation marks (" "). The following command

```
rsh sneezy cat file1 ">>" file2
```

will append the contents of file1 on the remote host **sneezy** to the current contents of file2 on the remote host. This entire command occurs exclusively on the remote host.

More than one command can be executed on the remote host using the ; operator. But since the metacharacter ; will be interpreted by the local shell, the whole string of commands must be enclosed in quotation marks. For example, the command

```
rsh sneezy "cd lowerdir;cat test2 >> test3"
```

will perform the concatenation operation in the subdirectory lowerdir of the Home directory of the user on the remote host **sneezy**. But the command

```
rsh sneezy cd lowerdir;cat test2 >> test3
```

will perform the concatenation operation in the current directory of the user on the local host and the specification of the **cd** command will be wasted.

If the **rsh** command is executed by itself with only the name of the remote host on the command line as in the following,

```
rsh sneezy
```

the **rlogin** command will be executed and a login into the remote host will be attempted. In addition, a set of aliases for the **/usr/ucb/rsh** executable can be created by executing commands such as

```
ln -s /usr/ucb/rsh sneezy
```

Then, when you enter just the name of the remote host of interest such as

```
sneezy
```

the actual command that is executed is

```
rsh sneezy
```

and the user will be logged automatically into **sneezy**.

Once you have the aliases defined, you can execute a command on a remote host just by entering the name of the host—for example, **sneezy**—and the command you want to execute on it. For example, the following

```
sneezy date
```

will execute the **date** command on the host **sneezy**.

The **rsh** command connects the standard input from the local command line as standard input to the remote command. Thus, input that is generated by one command can be piped using the pipeline (|) operation into an **rsh** command and have that generated output as input to the execution of the command on the remote host. Thus, the following command using a pipeline (|) operation

```
tar cvf - .  | rsh sneezy tar xvf -
```

will create a tar output file on the local host on standard output which is in turn tied to standard input for the **tar** command being run on the remote host **sneezy**. This command has the effect of copying files from one directory on one host into a directory on another host while preserving the subdirectory structure.

During the execution of the **rsh** command, after the connection to the remote host has been established but before the command is executed, the shell environment is created just as if you had logged in. Thus, if you use the Korn shell as your shell program on the remote host, the .profile script will be executed before the command you requested is executed. All the environment variables that you define in your user environment will be available to you to use in your command that is executed on that remote host.

While the command on the remote host is executing, a user can interrupt the processing or cause it to halt by entering the appropriate control character sequence. When the remote command terminates, the local **rsh** command will terminate also.

Interactive commands cannot be executed using an **rsh** command because input to the command must be specified on the command line.

Unlike some other remote commands such as **ftp**, the **rsh** command can be executed using a user id that has no password. Unfortunately, setting up such users violates the security of a system and is usually not done.

For a number of UNIX implementations, the command to execute single commands on a remote host may not be **rsh**, but instead may be **rcmd** (SCO UNIX, DG-UX, NCR UNIX) or **rexec**

(HP-UX). Examination of the manual pages for the UNIX system of interest should provide the name of the command to use.

 PITFALLS TO AVOID

Output from a command executed on the remote system will be sent back to the local host. If this command is executed in a background mode, the remote command will halt if the command can not write its output onto a terminal.

Special characters such as redirection (>>) or metacharacters such as *.{,}, and so forth, that have meaning to the various shell programs, will be interpreted on the local system and not on the remote system as desired. The user needs to make sure that these special characters are interpreted and acted upon on the particular host that the user has in mind. If the user wants these special characters to be interpreted on the local host, nothing needs to be done. If the user wants these special characters to be interpreted on the remote host, then they need to be enclosed in quotation marks (" ").

The local user may not be known on the remote system. This type of problem will lead to the user being denied access to the remote system. One approach to this problem is to use the -i option to specify the name of a user who is known on the remote system.

The local host may not be properly defined on the remote system in the various network tables, particularly the /etc/hosts.equiv file. Chapter 12 discusses this file in more detail. Failure to include the name of the remote host in the /etc/hosts.equiv will result in the local system being denied access to the remote system.

PC CONSIDERATIONS

Personal computer implementations of the **rsh** command do not seem to exist. When executing the **rsh** command from one host to another host, the target host must determine the name of the user on the source host. Most PC implementations of TCP/IP commands do not require that users log onto their PCs before using these commands. Thus, the name of the user is not known. The other TCP/IP commands that the PC has—**rlogin**, **telnet**, and **ftp**—require that the user be identified to the remote system by logging into the remote system and entering a user id and password. The **rsh** command requires that the source host identify itself and, thus, no PC implementation would be possible without requiring that users sign into their PC before using these commands.

INTERNET CONSIDERATIONS

The Internet does not support the **rsh** command. In order to execute commands on another host in the Internet, the user will have to log into that system using either the **rlogin** or **telnet** command.

BEHIND THE SCENES

The validation that the **rsh** server does is the same as the validation that is performed for the **rcp** command. In fact, the **rsh** server (normally called **rshd**) services both the **rsh** and **rcp** commands.

The remote host allows access only if at least one of the following conditions is true:

1. The local user is not the root user and the name of the local host is listed as an equivalent host in the /etc/hosts.equiv file on the remote system.
2. The remote user's Home directory (as defined in the /etc/passwd file) contains an .rhosts file that lists the local host and the local user name. For security reasons the .rhosts file must be readable by either the remote user or root and only the owner should have read and write access. In some implementations, if the permissions on the .rhosts file are not read/write only by owner, the file will be ignored and the request will be rejected.

In addition to the previous conditions, the **rsh** server validates the port number of the requesting process to ensure it is a system request.

If the command is not allowed because the user does not have the privilege to execute the command on the remote host, the command will be rejected by the remote host even if the user has the privilege to execute the command on the local host. Standard error is transmitted back to the local host over a separate connection between the local host and the remote host.

SUMMARY

Executing single commands on a remote host without logging in can be performed by using the **rsh** command. Any valid command that the user has the privilege to execute on the remote system can be run. Output from the command is returned to the originating host. Options allow the specification of a user name different from the user name on the local host and redirection of output into a file.

If you want to copy a file from one system to another, use the **rcp** command. But if you want to execute any other command, you would use the **rsh** command.

For further information on the **rsh** command or the **rshd** server, the user can examine the manual pages on the particular UNIX system of interest.

tftp Command:
Simple File Transfer

6

INTRODUCTION

Transferring single files between hosts of possibly dissimilar file systems (such as UNIX and VMS) can be accomplished using the **tftp** command. The **tftp** command is only meant for transferring one file at a time and does not provide many of the features that the **ftp** command provides (described in Chapter 7). For example, **tftp** does not support listing remote files or changing directories at the remote host site. **tftp** uses UDP as its transport protocol which, while providing less services, simplifies the implementation of the command. Thus, **tftp** services are suitable for loading diskless workstations.

This chapter will examine the **tftp** command, what problems can occur when executing **tftp** commands, using the **tftp** command on the personal computer, using the **tftp** command on the Internet, and how the server that supports the **tftp** command operates.

GETTING STARTED WITH THE tftp COMMAND

The **tftp** command can be used in two different forms: interactive form and command-line form. In command-line form, all of

the options for either command can be specified on the command line.

To operate the **tftp** command in the interactive mode, the command can be issued alone as in

```
tftp
```

once you do that, the interactive prompt

```
tftp>
```

is displayed. To transfer files, you would issue a **get** or **put** command specifying both the filename on the local host and the filename on the remote host. You can issue a series of **get** and **put** commands in one **tftp** session.

When data is transferred to a remote host, the transferred data is placed in the directory specified by the remfile parameter which must be a fully specified filename and the remote file must both exist and have write permissions set for others.

In the interactive mode, all of the various reading and writing functions can be used; reading and writing files are requested via the **get** and **put** commands. The host name can be specified in the **get** or **put** command. For example,

```
tftp> get sneezy:/etc/hosts /tmp/hosts
```

will copy from **sneezy** the /etc/hosts file and save it on the local host as /tmp/hosts. As another example, the command

```
tftp> put /etc/hosts sneezy:/etc/hosts
```

which will replace /etc/hosts file on **sneezy**. While in the interactive mode, you can use the **status** command to determine which host you will be accessing.

The command-line format provides command-line flags to specify all of the various functions for which you can use the **tftp** command. The **tftp** command with its options is described in Figure 6.1. With all of the options specifiable on the command line, shell scripts to move files from one system to another can be constructed and executed by the **cron** facility. One note: If

```
tftp {-p or -g} localfile host port remotefile {transfer type}
```
where:

`-p`	Indicates that the contents of *localfile* will be written to the *remotefile* filename on remote host
`-g`	Indicates that the contents of *remotefile* will be read from the remote host and written to *localfile*
`localfile`	Name of the file on local system to read data into or write data from
`host`	Name of the remote host to communicate with
`port`	Port number to use on the remote host
`remotefile`	Name of the file on remote system to write data into or read data from
`{transfer type}`	Specifies whether data is 7-bit ASCII-like or 8-bit Binary

FIGURE 6.1   **tftp** command and its options.

the file already exits on the local host, the **tftp** command will prompt before overwriting the already existing file.

Copying a file from one system to another is the main use of the **tftp** command. For example, the command

```
tftp -g newbook1 sneezy /u/fred/book1
```

will copy file /u/fred/book1 on host **sneezy** to the local host and save it as newbook1.

You can copy a file onto another system with

```
tftp -p /u/fred/test grumpy /tmp/test
```

which will copy file /u/fred/test onto **grumpy** as file /tmp/test.

 ADVANCED TIPS AND TECHNIQUES

Copying a file from one system to another is the main use of the **tftp** command. For example, the command

```
tftp -p file_to_run sneezy /tmp/file_to_run
```

will copy file file_to_run from the local host to the host **sneezy** and save it as /tmp/file_to_run. The host **sneezy** might not be a UNIX host but instead might be a terminal server or diskless workstation. The host that is executing the **tftp** program does not know much about the receiving host, only that the host acknowledged receiving the file. The receiving host does not have to perform many operations to receive this file from the sending host. In addition, the **tftp** command has very few options. Thus, the **tftp** command is simple to implement to use as a method of downloading terminal servers or diskless workstations.

You can specify a dash (-) as the name of the local file; when reading from a remote host, the output will be written to standard output. For example,

```
tftp -g - sneezy /etc/hosts
```

will display on your terminal the contents of the /etc/hosts file from the remote host **sneezy**.

You can specify a dash (-) as the name of the local file; when writing to a remote host, the **tftp** command will read input from standard input to be sent to the remote host. For example, the command

```
tftp -p - sneezy /etc/somehosts
```

will enable you to enter from the command data that you want to have stored in the /etc/somehosts on the remote host **sneezy**.

Output from the **tftp** command can be piped into another command. For example, the command

```
tftp -g - grumpy /etc/hosts | grep sneezy
```

would check that **sneezy** is defined in the /etc/hosts file on **grumpy**.

The **tftp** command uses the UDP protocol and not the TCP protocol. Generally, the UDP protocol is used so that a connection between the two hosts is not needed but the **tftp** command does form a connection to the remote host, but only for the duration of the transfer. In addition, there is no authentication of whether the request the **tftp** command is making is valid for this user. This command is suitable for downloading diskless workstations and terminal servers because all that needs to be known about the device to be downloaded is the address of the device to download (the port number is well-known).

PITFALLS TO AVOID

Because this is a simple command, there are only a few possible errors that can occur. These are listed with the error code and an explanation of the error in Figure 6.2. All of these error codes are fatal and will cause the transfer to be terminated. In addition, the error packet is not acknowledged or retransmitted and may not be received. But in any event no further transmissions will take place.

Error Code	Error Message	Meaning of Error Message
0	Not defined	Look at error message for explanation
1	File not found	Filename is not valid
2	Access violation	Denied access to file
3	Disk full	No room on disk for file
4	Illegal **tftp** operation	
5	Unknown port number	
6	File already exists	**tftp** will not overwrite a file that already exists
7	No such user	User's name not known to remote system

FIGURE 6.2 Possible error codes during **tftp** transfers.

PC CONSIDERATIONS

TCP/IP software for personal computers does not include implementations of the **tftp** command. Other commands, such as **ftp**, are available to copy files from one host to another.

INTERNET CONSIDERATIONS

Hosts on the Internet do not support **tftp** commands from outside their local networks. Other commands such as **ftp** are available to copy files from one host to another, so there is no need for Internet support of **tftp**. The TCP/IP transactions that the **tftp** command uses are not passed through network routers without special configuration of the router.

BEHIND THE SCENES

The **tftp** command uses UDP as its protocol because it is simple to implement. For devices that will be downloaded from a host such as diskless X terminals or terminal servers, the only function that the command provides is to copy onto the device the program that device will execute. A simple protocol will make the initial program that these devices execute smaller and easier to create. As shown in Figure 6.3, the **tftp** command acts as a client process and communicates with the **tftp** server on the remote host to request the service desired. The connection is only for the duration of the data exchange. Any error will cause the connection to be closed.

The five types of message packets are illustrated in Figure 6.4. The READ REQUEST and WRITE REQUEST packets contain a file name in ASCII text (terminated with \000) which is the name of the file to transfer. In addition, this packet also contains the format specifier: octet or netascii in the mode field. This packet is used to initiate the transfer of data and must be the first packet sent.

The DATA packet contains the block of data being transferred and includes a Block Number. Each packet contains

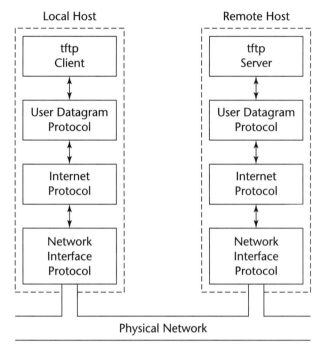

Local Host   Remote Host

FIGURE 6.3 **tftp** interaction with other TCP/IP protocols.

exactly 512 bytes, except for the last block which must contain less than 512 bytes. This last block in the file initiates the disconnect sequence.

The ACKNOWLEDGMENT packet acknowledges the receipt of a block and contains the number of the block which it is acknowledging. The numbering of blocks is sequential and the first block of data transferred is block number 1. Each block must be successfully acknowledged before another block will be sent.

The ERROR packet contains the error code and optional message indicating the error condition.

The connection to the remote host is initiated by sending the READ REQUEST or WRITE REQUEST to the well-known port address (69) of the **tftp** server on the remote host. The port number of the requester is chosen by the requesting process and should be randomized to avoid using the same port numbers in immediate succession.

Type of message

Layout of Message

	2 Bytes	String	1 Byte	String	1 Byte
READ REQUEST (RRQ)	01	Name of File	0	Mode	0

	2 Bytes	String	1 Byte	String	1 Byte
WRITE REQUEST (WRQ)	02	Name of File	0	Mode	0

	2 Bytes	2 Bytes	Up to 512 Bytes
DATA	03	Block #	Data

	2 Bytes	2 Bytes
ACK	04	Block #

	2 Bytes	2 Bytes	String	1 Byte
ERROR	05	ErrorCode	Error Message	0

FIGURE 6.4   Different **tftp** message types.

When the **tftp** server on the remote host receives the request, it will choose a new port number for itself, again in random sequence. Thus, the well-known port number for the **tftp** server is freed up so that another request can be serviced. The UDP packet contains the port number that the requesting process has chosen so that a reply to that process can be sent correctly addressed. The first reply to the initial request thus contains the port number to which all subsequent data packets (or acknowledgments for a write request) should be sent. Thus, the port number of the **tftp** server is used to send requests to, while two other ports are used for the actual data transfer that has been requested. Each receipt of another packet must be checked to be sure that the correct port number sent that packet, since port numbers are being used randomly and are not reserved for just the tftp requests. When the last block has been received and acknowledged, the connection can be terminated.

Closing a connection has no particular sequence of responses. When the transfer is done, the connection will be closed. The **tftp** server can drop the connection as soon as the last block is sent, although it should wait for the last acknowl-edgment to be received. The tftp requester does not know that the acknowledgment was received; but, as long as it successfully received all of the blocks in the file, it will not matter if the acknowledgment is received by the **tftp** server.

SUMMARY

The **tftp** command is a simple file transfer command that can be used to download diskless X terminals or terminal servers. Only the reading and writing of files are supported functions.

For further information on the **tftp** command, examine the manual page that is available on your favorite UNIX system. For more information on the tftp protocol, look at RFC 1350.

7

ftp Command: Transferring Files between Hosts

INTRODUCTION

The File Transfer (**ftp**) command is used to transfer files between hosts of possibly dissimilar file systems (such as UNIX versus VMS). Any kind of file can be transferred. One restriction that ftp imposes is that the user that is executing the **ftp** command must be known to the remote host and must have a password defined for it. (Some systems allow the use of the user *anonymous* which might not have a password and provide a special area for files that this user can access.) Thus, the use of the **ftp** command is fairly secure even though any readable file on a system can be retrieved by the **ftp** command.

The **ftp** command operates in an interactive mode which involves the user establishing a connection with the **ftp** server on the remote system using the TCP protocol. The ftp establishes two connections between the client and the server, one for control information such as commands and responses, and a second for transferring data. The interactive user will be prompted for a user name and password to establish the connection with the remote system. Once the connection is established, both text and binary files can be transferred.

This chapter will examine how to use the **ftp** command, what problems can occur when executing **ftp** commands, using the **ftp** command on the personal computer, using the **ftp** command on the Internet, and how the server that supports the **ftp** command operates.

GETTING STARTED WITH THE ftp COMMAND

If you just issue the **ftp** command by itself as in

```
ftp
```

the reply will be

```
ftp>
```

If you need assistance remembering what commands are available, you can enter **help** or **?** and you will have displayed on your terminal:

```
Commands may be abbreviated. Commands are:
!            delete       mdelete      proxy        runique
$            debug        mdir         sendport     send
account      dir          mget         put          size
append       disconnect   mkdir        pwd          status
ascii        form         mls          quit         struct
bell         get          mode         quote        sunique
binary       glob         modtime      recv         system
bye          hash         mput         remotehelp   tenex
case         help         nmap         rstatus      trace
cd           image        nlist        rhelp        type
cdup         lcd          ntrans       rename       user
close        ls           open         reset        verbose
cr           macdef       prompt       rmdir        ?
```

Then an ftp prompt would again be displayed. The next command you would normally enter is **open sneezy** to connect to **sneezy**. After you enter your user id and password, you would be ready to do file operations.

If the user wanted to specify the name of the host to connect to on the command line, the user would give the command

```
ftp nis.nsf.net
```

which would attempt to connect to the host named **nis.nsf.net**. If the connection is successful, a message such as

```
Connected to nis.nsf.net.
```

will appear. The **ftp** server on the remote host will usually send back a set of opening messages such as:

```
220-*****Welcome to the Network Information Center*****
    *****Login with username "anonymous" and password
  "guest"
  *****You may change directories to the following:
    ddn-news            - DDN Management Bulletins
    domain              - Root Domain Zone Files
    iesg                - IETF Steering Group
    ietf                - Internet Engineering Task Force
    internet-drafts     - Internet Drafts
    netinfo             - NIC Information Files
    netprog             - Guest Software (ex. whois.c)
    protocols           - TCP-IP & OSI Documents
    rfc                 - RFC Repository
    scc                 - DDN Security Bulletins
    std                 - Internet Protocol Standards
220 And more!
```

Finally, the **ftp** server on that host will ask for your name with the message

```
Name (nis.nsf.net:fred):
```

to which the user would answer with his or her name. For a login as a quest, you would answer: *anonymous*. (See a later section in this chapter for a discussion of what facilities ftp provides for public access to a system.) The remote **ftp** server would then prompt you for a password with the messages

```
331 Guest login ok, send "guest" as password.
 Password:
```

You would then reply with the appropriate password which for a public access would be *guest*. If this login sequence is accepted, the remote **ftp** server would give the message

```
230 Guest login ok, access restrictions apply.
```

Now the user is ready to transfer files. First the user might want to change to a directory where the files of interest are and ask for a list of the files in that directory:

```
cd netprog
ls
```

To which the **ftp** server would reply with a list of files:

```
200 PORT command successful.
150 Opening ASCII mode data connection for file list.
whois.c.old
whois.c
nicusr.fai
nicname.c
00netprog-index.txt
dns-software.txt
226 Transfer complete.
```

Then the local ftp client would again display the ftp prompt *ftp>*. If the user wanted to transfer the file 00netprogindex.txt, he would enter the command

```
get 00netprog-index.txt
```

and the replies would be

```
200 PORT command successful.
150 Opening ASCII mode data connection for
      00netprog- index.txt (567 bytes).
226 Transfer complete.
578 bytes received in 0.2343 seconds (2.409 Kbytes/s)
```

```
ftp> cd ../fyi
250 CWD command successful.
ftp> get INDEX.fyi
200 PORT command successful.
150 Opening ASCII mode data connection for INDEX.fyi (5867 bytes).
226 Transfer complete.
5996 bytes received in 0.1843 seconds (31.78 Kbytes/s)
ftp> ls *INDEX*.*
200 PORT command successful.
150 Opening ASCII mode data connection for file list.
fyi-index.txt
rfc-index.txt
226 Transfer complete.
ftp> get INDEX.rfc
200 PORT command successful.
150 Opening ASCII mode data connection for INDEX.rfc (168866
bytes).
226 Transfer complete.
173092 bytes received in 7.725 seconds (21.88 Kbytes/s)
ftp>
```

FIGURE 7.1   Dialogue during an **ftp** transfer of two files.

The ftp prompt would be displayed indicating that another command could be entered. Figure 7.1 is the dialogue that would ensue if the user wanted to transfer two files INDEX.fyi and INDEX.rfc from the fyi directory. After the user has transferred the files of interest and wants to end the session, he or she would enter the command **quit** and the connection would be ended.

ADVANCED TIPS AND TECHNIQUES

The **ftp** command provides a rich set of file manipulation commands which can be grouped into the following categories:

Transferring and managing files

Listing and changing contents of directories

Managing which files will be transferred

Managing connections with remote hosts

Managing the characteristics of files being transferred

Managing miscellaneous commands

Command-line arguments for the **ftp** command

Each of these groups of commands will be addressed in the following sections. One note when specifying these commands: Any part of the command which is enclosed in brackets ([ ]) is optional.

Transferring and Managing Files

Since one of the major functions of the **ftp** command is to transfer files, the **ftp** command provides a large number of commands to facilitate transferring and managing the files that were transferred as summarized in Figure 7.2. (As a note, the naming of files on the local host and remote hosts is affected by the setting of the ntrans and nmap options.)

* **append LocalFile [RemoteFile]** will transfer LocalFile to the remote system and will add its contents to the current contents of RemoteFile if it is specified and exists or will add

ftp Command	Action
append LocalFile [RemoteFile]	Add contents of LocalFile to RemoteFile
delete RemoteFile	Delete RemoteFile
get RemoteFile [LocalFile]	Retrieve contents of RemoteFile
mdelete RemoteFiles	Delete RemoteFile(s)
mget RemoteFiles	Retrieve contents of RemoteFile(s)
mput [LocalFiles]	Transfer Contents of LocalFile(s)
put LocalFile [RemoteFile]	Transfer LocalFile
recv RemoteFile [LocalFile]	Retrieve contents of RemoteFile
rename FromName ToName	Rename File on Remote System
send LocalFile [RemoteFile]	Transfer LocalFile

FIGURE 7.2 ftp commands to transfer and manage files.

its contents to the LocalFile (on the remote system) if it exists. If neither RemoteFile is specified nor does LocalFile exist, LocalFile will be created and will contain whatever LocalFile contained on the local host.

- **delete RemoteFile** will delete the file named RemoteFile on the remote system if it exists.
- **get RemoteFile [LocalFile]** and **recv RemoteFile [LocalFile]** will transfer the file RemoteFile from the remote host to the local host and will name that file LocalFile if LocalFile has been specified or RemoteFile if LocalFile was not specified.
- **mdelete RemoteFiles** will delete the group of files whose names are generated by the expansion of the RemoteFiles specification.
- **mget RemoteFiles** will transfer the set of files specified by RemoteFiles from the remote host to the local host and retain their original names on the local host. Usually the specification RemoteFiles contains special characters to indicate what group of files is intended to be transferred. These special characters such as *, {, and so forth are often called *metacharacters* and are interpreted just as the C shell would.
- **mput [LocalFiles]** will transfer the group of LocalFiles to the remote host and name them the same as modified by the setting of ntrans and nmap options.
- **put LocalFile [RemoteFile]** and **send LocalFile [RemoteFile]** will transfer the contents of the file named LocalFile from the local system to the remote system and will name the file RemoteFile if a name is specified or will name the file LocalFile if RemoteFile is not specified. The filename on the remote host will be modified by the setting of ntrans and nmap options.
- **rename FromName ToName** will rename the file named FromName to a file named ToName on the remote system.

Listing and Changing Contents of Directories

The following commands are for managing the directory to which you are transferring files or from which you are transferring files. Figure 7.3 summarizes how these commands operate.

ftp Command	Action
lcd [Directory]	Changes local working directory
mdir [RemoteDirectories LocalFile]	Lists contents of *RemoteDirectories* into *LocalFile*
mkdir RemoteDirectory	Creates the directory *RemoteDirectory*
mls [RemoteDirectories LocalFile]	Lists contents of *RemoteDirectories* into *LocalFile*
nlist	Lists contents of a directory
pwd	Displays the name of the current directory
rmdir RemoteDirectory	Removes the directory *RemoteDirectory*
size Filename	Returns the size of *Filename*

FIGURE 7.3 ftp commands to change and list directories.

- **cd RemoteDirectory** will change the current working directory on the remote system to be RemoteDirectory.
- **cdup** will move up one level in the directory tree on the remote system.
- **dir [RemoteDirectory] [LocalFile]** or **ls [RemoteDirectory] [LocalFile]** writes a listing of the contents of the RemoteDirectory into LocalFile on the local host. If the LocalFile is not specified, the listing of the contents of the RemoteDirectory are displayed on the local terminal. If the RemoteDirectory is not specified, a listing of the current directory is displayed on the local terminal.
- **lcd [Directory]** changes the working directory on the local host to Directory.
- **mdir [RemoteDirectories LocalFile]** or **mls [RemoteDirectories LocalFile]** writes a listing of the contents of the set of directories to which RemoteDirectories expands to the LocalFile file if it is specified or to the local terminal if LocalFile is a hyphen (-). If LocalFile is not specified, the name of a local file will be prompted for. RemoteDirectories may contain metacharacters and/or pattern-matching characters. Remote-

Directories may contain a list of remote directories separated by blanks.

- **mkdir RemoteDirectory** will create the directory Remote-Directory on the remote host.
- **nlist** prints a list of the files of a directory on the remote host.
- **pwd** displays the name of the current directory on the remote host.
- **rmdir RemoteDirectory** removes the directory RemoteDirectory from the remote host.
- **size Filename** returns the size of Filename on the remote machine in bytes.

Managing Which File(s) Will Be Transferred

Often users want to transfer a group of files; therefore, it would be advantageous to be able to specify a group of files to be transferred. In addition, when transferring files between two dissimilar file systems, it may be important to modify the name of the transferred files to fit the syntax of the target system. The following commands enable the user to specify some naming options. These options are listed in Figure 7.4 and can be used to adjust the names of files that are being transferred from some systems that use only uppercase filenames to lowercase names. Further, on some systems extensions may be different.

ftp Command	*Action*
case	Convert filenames to lowercase (or not)
glob	Expand filenames (or not)
nmap [InPattern OutPattern]	Map filenames using patterns
ntrans [InCharacter [OutCharacter]]	Translate filenames
runique	Create unique filenames during get or mget operations (or not)
sunique	Create unique filenames during put or mput operations (or not)

FIGURE 7.4 **ftp** commands to manage which files will be transferred.

- **case** is a toggle that, when it is on, will cause remote filenames that are displayed in uppercase letters to be changed to lowercase letters when these files are created on the local system.
- **glob** is a toggle that, when it is on, will cause the expansion of filenames for the **mget**, **mput**, and **mdelete** commands. When it is off, it will suppress expansion of filenames.
- **nmap [InPattern OutPattern]** enables filename mapping with any occurrence of InPattern changed to OutPattern. This option can be used to specify the naming of destination files during **mput** or **put** operations or source files during **mget** or **get** operations.
- **ntrans [InCharacter [OutCharacter]]** enables filename character translation with InCharacter(s) replaced by OutCharacter(s) for source filenames or destination filenames.
- **runique** causes unique filenames to be created for local destination files during **get** and **mget** subcommands. If a local destination filename already exists, a unique name will be created adding .1 to the usual destination filename. If that name already exists, the number is incremented until a unique name is generated.
- **sunique** causes unique filenames to be created for remote destination files during **put** and **mput** subcommands. If a remote destination filename already exists, a unique name will be created adding .1 to the usual destination filename. If that name already exists, the number is incremented until a unique name is generated.

Managing Connections with Remote Hosts

The **ftp** command provides a number of ways to control which remote host you are connected to and what your user name and password for that remote host might be. These commands are summarized in Figure 7.5.

- **account [Password]** sends a supplemental password that a remote host may require before allowing access to certain resources.
- **bye** or **quit** ends the ftp session and exits the command.
- **close** or **disconnect** ends the ftp session but does not exit the **ftp** command. The ftp prompt will be displayed next.

ftp Command	*Action*
`account [Password]`	Send a supplemental password
`bye`	End ftp session and command
`close`	Close connection with remote host but continue ftp command
`disconnect`	Same as close
`open HostName [Port]`	Establish connection with remote host `HostName`, optionally on port `Port`
`quit`	End ftp session and command
`sendport`	Allow `Port` command or not
`user User [Password] [Account]`	Identify `User` to remote host optionally with password `Password` and account `Account`

FIGURE 7.5 **ftp** commands to manage user login and password.

- **open HostName [Port]** establishes a connection to the **ftp** server on HostName. If the port is specified, the connection to a server will be at that port. If autologin is set, the **ftp** command will attempt to automatically log the user into the **ftp** server. (The file .netrc must exist in the user's Home directory with the correct information before autologin will succeed.)
- **sendport** is a toggle which controls the use of Port **ftp** command.
- **user User [Password] [Account]** identifies the local user as User to the remote **ftp** server. If password or account is required by the remote server, either can be specified here.

Managing the Characteristics of Files Being Transferred

Some commands (listed in Figure 7.6) enable the user to manage the characteristics of files being transferred.

- **ascii** sets the file transfer type to network ASCII.
- **binary** sets the file transfer type to binary image.
- **cr** strips carriage return character from a carriage return and

ftp Command	Action
ascii	Sets transfer type to ASCII
binary	Sets transfer type to binary
cr	Strips carriage returns from a carriage return and line feed sequence (or not)
form	Sets form of file transfer
mode	Sets mode of file transfer
struct	Sets structure of file transfer
tenex	Sets transfer type to TENEX
type [Type]	Sets transfer type to Type

FIGURE 7.6 **ftp** commands to manage the characteristics of files.

line-feed sequence when receiving records during ASCII-type file transfers. This option is useful when transferring files from a DOS system to a UNIX system.

- **form** specifies form of the file transfer and the only form available is file.
- **mode** sets file transfer mode but the only mode available is stream.
- **struct** sets data transfer structure type and the only available structure is stream.
- **tenex** sets file transfer type to that needed by TENEX machines.
- **type [Type]** sets file transfer type to Type; choices are ASCII or binary.

Managing Miscellaneous Commands

Some commands do not fall into any easily definable category. These commands are summarized in Figure 7.7.

- **bell** sounds a bell after each file transfer is completed.
- **! [Command] [Parameters]** invokes an interactive shell on

ftp Command	*Action*
`bell`	Sounds a bell after transfer is complete
`! [Command] [Parameters]`	Exits to shell and optionally execute command `Command` with parameters `Parameters`
`? [Subcommand]`	Displays help or help on subcommand `Subcommand`
`debug`	Displays each command sent to host (or not)
`hash`	Prints a # for each 1,024 bytes transferred (or not)
`help`	Displays information on commands
`macdef`	Defines a subcommand macro
`modtime`	Displays modification time of file on remote host
`prompt`	Prompts interactively (or not)
`proxy [Subcommand]`	Executes command on a secondary connection
`remotehelp [Subcommand]`	Displays help on command on remote host
`reset`	Clears reply queue
`status`	Displays status of `ftp` command
`system`	Displays type of system remote host is
`trace`	Traces packets (or not)
`verbose`	Displays responses from remote host (or not)

FIGURE 7.7 **ftp** commands for miscellaneous tasks.

the local host and will execute Command if it is specified with Parameters if they are specified.

- **? [Subcommand]** displays a description of Subcommand or a list of available subcommands if Subcommand is not specified.
- **debug** toggles whether each command that is sent to the remote host will be printed (on is the default).
- **hash** toggles whether one hash sign (7 - #) will be printed for each 1,024 bytes that are transferred.

- **help** displays help information.
- **macdef** defines a subcommand macro.
- **modtime Filename** displays the last modification time of file **Filename** on the remote system.
- **prompt** toggles interactive prompting. If interactive prompting is on (the default), the **ftp** command will prompt before retrieving, sending, or deleting multiple files during **mget**, **mput**, and **mdelete** subcommands.
- **proxy [Subcommand]** executes an **ftp** command on a second control connection. Thus, this command can be used to establish a connection to a second remote host to enable transferring files between the two remote hosts. The first command that should be executed under a proxy account should be an **open** subcommand. A list of **proxy** subcommands can be obtained by executing a **proxy ?** subcommand.
- **remotehelp [Subcommand]** requests help from the remote **ftp** server. If Subcommand is specified, only information about that subcommand will be displayed; otherwise, a list of commands (at the minimum) will be displayed.
- **reset** clears the reply queue and resynchronizes the command parsing.
- **status** displays current status of the **ftp** command. For example, when you are connected to another machine and enter the command **status** you would get the response:

```
Connected to nic.ddn.mil.
 No proxy connection.
 Mode: stream; Type: ascii; Form: non-print; Structure: file
 Verbose: on; Bell: off; Prompting: on; Globbing: on
 Store unique: off; Receive unique: off
 Case: off; CR stripping: on
 Ntrans: off
 Nmap: off
 Hash mark printing: off; Use of PORT cmds: on
 Experimental commands: off
```

- **system** shows the type of operating system on the remote system. For example, if you are connected to another UNIX machine, you might get a response of:

```
215 UNIX Type: L8 Version: BSD-44
```

- **trace** toggles packet tracing.
- **verbose** toggles verbose mode (default is on) which will display all responses from the remote server.

Command-line Arguments for the ftp Command

Some options for the **ftp** command which can be specified by subcommands can also be specified via command-line arguments. These command-line options are shown in Figure 7.8. For example, the name of the host that the **ftp** command is to connect to can be specified in an **open** subcommand and can also be specified on the command line. For example, the following command

```
ftp snoopy
```

will cause the **ftp** command to establish a connection with the host **snoopy**.

Displaying output that could be used for debugging problems which can be enabled by issuing the **debug** subcommand can be enabled by including the -d option on the command line. Disabling expansion of metacharacters in filenames can be controlled by the **glob** subcommand and also by specifying the -g option on the command line. Disabling interactive prompting during multiple file transfers can be controlled by the **prompt** subcommand and also by specifying the -i option on the command line. Specifying the -v option on the command line will

ftp Command	Action
Line Option	
-d	Debug mode
-g	Disable filename expansion
-i	Disable interactive prompting during file transfers
-n	Suppress automatic logging into remote system
-v	Verbose mode

FIGURE 7.8 ftp command line options.

```
#!/bin/csh -f
#
#   Parameter is number of RFC to retrieve
#
#   (Use of $$ described in C shell Chapter)
echo "" >> /tmp/$$M
#  Send user name and password
echo "user anonymous marick@mycompany.com"
                                    >> /tmp/$$M
#  Get into directory of interest
echo "cd internet/documents/fyi" >> /tmp/$$M
echo "get INDEX.fyi" >> /tmp/$$M
echo "cd ../rfc" >> /tmp/$$M
echo "get INDEX.rfc" >> /tmp/$$M
while ( $#argv > 0 )
     echo "get rfc$1.txt" >> /tmp/$$M
     shift
end
echo "quit" >> /tmp/$$M
ftp -nv nis.nsf.net < /tmp/$$M >& ftp.out
sleep 10
rm /tmp/$$M
#
```

FIGURE 7.9   C shell script to transfer files.

display all the responses from the remote server and provide data transfer statistics. Normally this is the default mode but, if output is being redirected to a file, the verbose mode is not in effect unless the -v option or the **verbose** subcommand is used.

Finally, there is one last option that is controlled by a command-line argument. If the user needs to suppress automatic logging in of the user on the remote system, the user can specify the -n option on the command line. This option is needed if the user wishes to connect to another host and perform file transfers under a different user id. (See the example on "Anonymous ftp Session".)

As discussed earlier in this chapter, it is possible to set up a file (.netrc) so that a user can automatically log into another

```
Connected to nis.nsf.net.
220 nic.merit.edu FTP server ... 14:33:38 EDT 1994) ready.
331 Guest login ok, send your email address as password.
230- Guest login ok, access restrictions apply.
230- Local time is: Sun Jan 15 10:53:26 1995
250 CWD command successful.
200 PORT command successful.
150 Opening ASCII mode data ... for INDEX.fyi (5422 bytes).
226 Transfer complete.
5565 bytes received in 0.709 seconds (7.665 Kbytes/s)
250 CWD command successful.
200 PORT command successful.
150 Opening ASCII mode ... for INDEX.rfc (290145 bytes).
226 Transfer complete.
296310 bytes received in 13.76 seconds (21.02 Kbytes/s)
200 PORT command successful.
150 Opening ASCII mode ... for rfc1349.txt (68949 bytes).
226 Transfer complete.
70573 bytes received in 3.292 seconds (20.93 Kbytes/s)
221 Goodbye.
```

FIGURE 7.10 Dialogue during file transfer using C shell script.

host. With this capability it is possible to build scripts of commands to transfer files without user intervention. Another possibility is to turn off automatically logging in and provide the name of the user and the password in the set of commands that are read in by the **ftp** command. Figure 7.9 is an example of a C shell script to transfer two files (INDEX.fyi and INDEX.rfc) and to transfer an RFC (rfcNN.txt) if NN is specified on the command line. For example, if the command that is entered on the command line is

```
ftp_comm 1349
```

the output that is generated is shown in Figure 7.10 which shows the user *anonymous* with password *guest* logging in on the host **nis.nsf.net** and then retrieving three files, INDEX.fyi, INDEX.rfc, and rfc1349.txt.

PITFALLS TO AVOID

One problem that can occur when transferring files using **ftp**, is the kind of file may not be preserved. If the file is an executable or a binary file, then you must inform **ftp** that you want to preserve the file as is by turning on the binary file option using the **binary** command. If you do not do that, **ftp** will not attempt to preserve the file in its original form. In fact, if the file is being transferred from a UNIX system to a DOS system, the **ftp** command will change every line feed to carriage return and line feed. For a binary file, this operation will corrupt the file and make it useless.

PC CONSIDERATIONS

The **ftp** command has been implemented for the personal computer in both DOS and Windows environments. In the DOS environment, the **ftp** implementations operate much like the earlier discussions in this chapter. You can specify the remote host to connect to on the command line; once connected, you will interact with that remote host issuing transfer commands as explained in the earlier part of this chapter.

In the Windows environment, the name of the host to connect to can often be specified as the name of the session to execute. Once the connection is made to the remote host, the files in the current directory on both the local host and remote host are displayed. To transfer a file, you highlight the file of interest and choose the appropriate copy button. The Windows application does the rest.

One added feature is that if you are transferring text files from a DOS system (or Windows system) to a UNIX system or vice versa, the **ftp** command will convert the format from the DOS text file format to the UNIX format or vice versa. This format conversion means that on a DOS system each line in a text file will end with both carriage return and line feed characters, while on a UNIX system each line will end with a line feed character only. In addition, DOS text files end with a Ctrl-Z character (^Z) while UNIX text files do not end with any special character.

Thus, the **ftp** command will convert carriage return—line-feed character pairs to just a single line-feed character when copying a file from a DOS system to a UNIX system. Carriage return characters will be added to each line of text file when copying the file from UNIX to DOS. This type of conversion will usually damage an executable file; thus, you must turn on the binary option before transferring binary files so that the file will not be converted.

INTERNET CONSIDERATIONS

When using the **ftp** command and connecting to a host, the user is required to provide a user id and a password. Thus, for a user to have access to a host, that user has to be defined on that system and a password must be set up for that user on that system. But suppose a group of people want to make a set of files available to the computing public on a particular host in their facility? If they had to define every user and provide a password for every user, they would not be very willing. Instead, the **ftp** command provides a special user id called *anonymous* which will accept any password and, thus, provides access by every user to all files that are in the Home directory of the ftp user. Then, to make files available to any user that uses this method to connect to your system, you would put the files that are public in that directory (or in a subdirectory in that directory). Sites that provide this availability are called *archive* sites.

Many systems on the Internet provide the anonymous method of transferring files so that they can provide extensive collections of data and files to the world at large. This Internet service provides the ability to transfer files between two sites on the Internet. The use of the **ftp** command to transfer files between dissimilar sites within a local network was discussed in Chapter 6. This same command can be used to transfer files between your host and an Internet host.

An example of an interactive **ftp** session using the *anonymous* user id is shown in Figure 7.11 where a connection has been made to the archive site named wuarchive.wustl.edu to retrieve some software. Following the naming conventions of

goofy:/usr/marty/save[6]% `ftp wuarchive.wustl.edu`
Connected to wuarchive.wustl.edu.
220 wuarchive.wustl.edu FTP server (Version wu-2.4(1) Mon Jul 8
11:53:55 CDT 1994) ready.

Name (wuarchive.wustl.edu:marty): `anonymous`
331 Guest login ok, send your complete e-mail address as password.

Password: `marick@mycompany.com`   (Not displayed)
230- If your FTP client crashes or hangs shortly after login
    (Some messages deleted)
230 Guest login ok, access restrictions apply.

ftp> `ls -C`
200 PORT command successful.
150 Opening ASCII mode data connection for /bin/ls.

README	decus	graphics	mirrors	pub
README.NFS	doc	index.html	multimedia	systems
bin	edu	info	packages	usenet
core	etc	languages	private	

226 Transfer complete.

ftp> `cd usenet`
250 CWD command successful.

ftp> `cd comp.binaries.ibm.pc`
250 CWD command successful.

ftp> `ls -C`
200 PORT command successful.
150 Opening ASCII mode data connection for /bin/ls.
Index volume03 volume07 volume11 volume15 volume19 volume23
volume00 volume04 volume08 volume12 volume16 volume20 volume24
volume01 volume05 volume09 volume13 volume17 volume21 volume25
volume02 volume06 volume10 volume14 volume18 volume22 volume26
226 Transfer complete.

ftp> `get Index Index.comp.binaries.ibm.pc`
200 PORT command successful.
150 Opening ASCII mode data connection for Index (31556 bytes).
226 Transfer complete.
31872 bytes received in 4.063 seconds (7.661 Kbytes/s)

ftp> `quit`
221 Goodbye.

FIGURE 7.11   Connecting as *anonymous* for file transfers.

the Internet, this Internet site is at a university, specifically at Washington University in St. Louis. As a courtesy, you use your Internet electronic mail address as the password so that the archive site can know the name of the users of their Internet site. While connected as the *anonymous* user, all of the directories and files in the Home directory of the *anonymous* user are available to retrieve files from or to put files into.

In this particular session, while connected to wuarchive. wustl.edu, the directories in the Home directory of the *anonymous* user were listed using the **ls** command. Then the working directory was changed to one that contains the files of interest with the command

```
cd comp.binaries.ibm.pc
```

Finally, a text listing of all the software in this archive was retrieved with the command

```
get Index Index.comp.binaries.ibm.pc
```

which transferred the Index file to the local system and named that file Index.comp.binaries.ibm.pc. After retrieving the listing of the contents of this archive site, we ended the **ftp** session. In general, archive sites maintain a file such as INDEX, index, or readme.txt that describes what the various files are that they are storing in this directory. A few of the better known archive sites are listed in Figure 7.12.

BEHIND THE SCENES

Ftp commands and replies are exchanged through one connection while data is transferred over a separate connection as shown in Figure 7.13. The ftp client communicates with the **ftp** server on the remote host using TCP as the intermediary protocol as shown in Figure 7.14. The ftp connection protocol follows the telnet protocol methodology. During transfers, the status of the data transfers can be determined at any time because separate connections are used. Even if the data transfer is aborted, the other connection allows status information to be exchanged. Thus, the connection for data transfer is temporary and transient.

Archive Site	Contents
rtfm.mit.edu	Usenet Frequently Asked Questions (FAQ) documents
aixpdslib.seas.ucla.edu	Public RS/6000 AIX Software
oak.oakland.edu wuarchive.wustl.edu	Public software for a wide range of operating systems
ftp.uu.net	Usenet FAQ documents Internet background documents
whitehouse.gov	Presidential position papers Press releases
gatekeeper.dec.com	Recipes from various Usenet groups Public X11 software
town.hall.org	Filings with the Securities and Exchange Commission
ftp.psi.com	Internet documents TCP/IP standards documents
mrcnext.cso.uiuc.edu	Full text of a variety of books (known as Project Gutenberg)
cs.uwp.edu	Information on classical music with a guide to CDs
ftp.ncsa.uiuc.edu	Public domain Mosaic
software.watson.ibm.com	IBM Watson Publications
ftp.microsoft.com	Microsoft public software and information

FIGURE 7.12 Some popular archive sites.

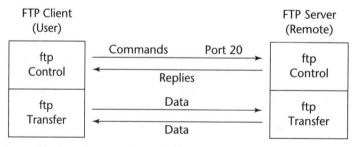

FIGURE 7.13 ftp client/server interaction.

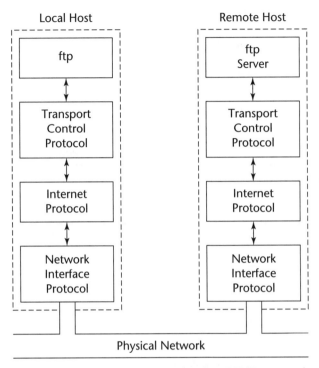

FIGURE 7.14   ftp interaction with other TCP/IP protocols.

All ftp commands are displayed with a reply message in mind. Thus, at any point in an ftp session the state of the user will be known. For example, sending the message "int" puts that user into the "waiting for reply" state; when the reply is received and finished, the user will be in the "wanting to send command:."

Some commands will receive more than one reply from the server but, since the reply messages are coded, the user can determine whether to expect another reply message. For the command **retrieve file**, the first reply is a "Positive Preliminary Reply" (100) indicating that the command is accepted and being processed.

What Do ftp Reply Messages Mean?

ftp commands are interactive in that every command will be followed by at least one line of reply message. Sometimes there will be several reply messages while the operation proceeds, but every command is followed by at least one reply.

Leading Digit in ftp Reply Codes	Meaning of Message
1yz	Positive preliminary reply
2yz	Positive completion reply
3yz	Positive intermediate reply
4yz	Transient negative completion reply
5yz	Permanent negative completion reply

FIGURE 7.15   Meaning of leading digit in ftp reply codes.

Middle Digit in ftp Reply Codes	Meaning of Message
x0z	Syntax errors
x1z	Informational message
x2z	Connection message
x3z	Authentication and accounting message
x4z	Not currently used
x5z	File system messages

FIGURE 7.16   Meaning of middle digit in ftp reply codes.

Replies to an **ftp** command have a particular format: The first field in the reply is a three-digit number called the reply code, followed by either a space or a minus sign, and then some text. The reply codes are designed to be read and analyzed by a process and thus follow a particular format. The first digit of the reply as listed in Figure 7.15 indicates how the request is being performed while the second digit of the reply code indicates what kind of error it is, as shown in Figure 7.16.

After the reply code there will be at least one line of text for human beings to read. If more than one line of reply is necessary, a minus sign in the first message line signals the existence of multiple lines of reply and the final line of reply begins with the error code. A full list of ftp reply codes is shown in Figure 7.17.

Code	Meaning of Message
110	Restart marker reply. In this case, the text is exact and not left to the particular implementation; it must read: MARK yyyy = mmmm Where yyyy is User-process data stream marker, and mmmm server's equivalent marker (note the spaces between markers and "=").
120	Service ready in nnn minutes.
125	Data connection already open; transfer starting.
150	File status okay; about to open data connection.
200	Command okay.
202	Command not implemented, superfluous at this site.
211	System status, or system help reply.
212	Directory status.
213	File status.
214	Help message. On how to use the server or the meaning of a particular non-standard command. This reply is useful only to the human user.
215	NAME system type. Where NAME is an official system name from the list in the Assigned Numbers document.
220	Service ready for new user.
221	Service closing control connection. Logged out if appropriate.
225	Data connection open; no transfer in progress.
226	Closing data connection. Requested file action successful (for example, file transfer or file abort).
227	Entering Passive Mode (h1,h2,h3,h4,p1,p2).
230	User logged in, proceed.
250	Requested file action okay, completed.
257	"PATHNAME" created.
331	User name okay, need password.
332	Need account for login.
350	Requested file action pending further information.

FIGURE 7.17 ftp reply codes in numeric order.

Code	Meaning of Message
421	Service not available, closing control connection. This may be a reply to any command if the service knows it must shut down.
425	Can't open data connection.
426	Connection closed; transfer aborted
450	Requested file action not taken. File unavailable (e.g., file busy).
451	Requested action aborted: local error in processing.
452	Requested action not taken. Insufficient storage space in system.
500	Syntax error, command unrecognized. This may include errors such as command line too long.
501	Syntax error in parameters or arguments.
502	Command not implemented.
503	Bad sequence of commands.
504	Command not implemented for that parameter.
530	Not logged in.
532	Need account for storing files.
550	Requested action not taken. File unavailable (e.g., file not found, no access).
551	Requested action aborted: page type unknown.
552	Requested file action aborted. Exceeded storage allocation (for current directory or dataset).
553	Requested action not taken. File name not allowed.

FIGURE 7.17　(Continued)

SUMMARY

The **ftp** command is used to transfer files between the local host and a remote host or between two remote hosts. Options can be specified to ensure that transferred files have unique file names. The names of files can be manipulated so that the naming conventions of the receiving host can be followed. Scripts can be created that will perform the file transfers for the user. Public access to files is provided via the anonymous login.

The standard TCP/IP file transfer facilities and how they function are described in RFC 959 titled "File Transfer Protocol" written by J. Postel and J. Reynolds in 1985. For further information on the **ftp** command itself, examine the manual pages on the UNIX system of interest.

mail Command: Electronic Mail Services

INTRODUCTION

One service that users desire is to be able to exchange messages with other users somewhere in the network. To make matters easier, users want to send a message to another user without knowing where that user is in the network. UNIX systems provide at least one basic command called **mail** to send mail to another user and to read mail. (Although personal computers (PCs) often have another set of software to read messages that other users have sent, these PC-based mail-reading programs are beyond the scope of this book and will not be covered.)

The hosts can be on different networks and so forth, but how do they set up the messages so that they can be delivered to the user on the system that is intended? Typical mail addresses are two-level: The first level is the name of the user and the second level is the name of the host using network names. The operation that enables mail to be delivered to another user is invisible to the user.

TCP/IP provides a protocol to exchange mail between users called Simple Mail Transfer Protocol (SMTP). The functionality of SMTP is designed to deliver mail reliably. SMTP is designed to work with any reliable byte stream and can be used on top of protocols other than TCP. This protocol enables even PC-based mail systems to send mail to users on UNIX systems and to receive mail from users on UNIX systems.

GETTING STARTED WITH THE mail COMMAND

Sending a message to another user and reading the messages from other users are at the heart of electronic messaging systems. The **mail** command provides the basic commands to accomplish both of these tasks.

Sending a Message to Another User

On a UNIX system to send mail to a user, you merely need to execute the **mail** command and specify the name of the person to whom you want to send a message on the command line as an option, as in

```
mail harry
```

which would start the **mail** command to create a message to send to the user *harry*. The cursor will be placed at the beginning of the next line but no prompt will be shown there. The **mail** command is waiting for you to type in your message. You can type in as long a message as you wish. When the message is complete, you indicate that fact to the **mail** command by pressing the Ctrl key and the D key at the beginning of a line.

Following the creation of your mail message, the **mail** command will prompt for whom to send carbon copies to with the cc: prompt. You can enter no names by pressing <Return> or just one name by typing that name in, or you could enter several names by stringing them on the same line separated by commas. Once you have completed your message, the sendmail demon will receive the message and forward that message to the host on which your addressee reads his or her mail.

The person to whom you have sent a message does not have to be logged onto the system. In fact, the person might actually be on a different host somewhere in your network. To send a message to such a person, you need to put the name of the host as part of the name of the person to whom the letter is addressed. The format of this network addressing is

```
harry@jbm.com
```

which would send the mail to the host **jbm.com** and deliver the mail to the user *harry* who is expected to be reading his mail there. (In fact, user *harry* could be reading his mail somewhere else. As long as the host **jbm.com** knows how to forward mail to *harry*, your message will be delivered.) If the address that you specify is not correct, the letter will be returned to you as an "Undeliverable message." If you specified the above address as just *harry*, the mail delivery system will expect to deliver the mail locally.

You can put a subject on your message by using the **-s** command option. This information is in the one-line entry displayed when you looked at the messages that you received from others. For example, the command

```
mail -s "Greetings from your pal SNOOPY" harry@jbm.com
```

will send mail to the user *harry* on system **jbm.com** and indicate that the subject is just a "Greetings" message. The **mail** command will then place you in input mode so that you can type in the message for harry@jbm.com. You should use as a subject something that will catch the user's attention and indicate whether this message needs to be read immediately. You probably would get a different response from *harry* if you sent the message

```
mail -s "Your Printer is on fire" harry
```

which would probably cause *harry* to check what his printer was doing. You don't need to add a message; you can use the subject as your message. You are not required to type in a message if you do not wish to. As another example, suppose you are trying to schedule a meeting; you might use the following command

```
mail -s "Operations mtg is 4PM Tuesday"
                              harry,fred,janice
```

The **mail** command will expect you to type in a message but you can just press <Ctrl> and D keys together and an empty message will be sent to each name on your list. The subject field contains the message so no message is needed.

Reading Your Messages

Other users can correspond with you, even if you are not currently on the system, by sending you mail. The **sendmail** server (discussed in a later section) transfers messages from one host to another until that message gets to a host on which the target user has a mail account. When you sign on to a UNIX system, you will be notified if there is mail for you with the message

```
You have mail
```

Now you can read the mail others have sent you by entering the **mail** command

```
mail
```

which gives you a list of the messages that you have not yet read such as

```
System V Mail Type ? for help.
"/usr/spool/mail/martya": 1 message 1 new
>N 1 martya Tue Nov 30 10:01 11/262 Good News
```

This indicates that you have one message. If you have no messages to read, the **mail** command will exit with the message

No mail in /usr/spool/mail/martya.

You can read your messages in succession just by touching the <Enter> key; the oldest unread message will be displayed. Thus, if you just touch the <Enter> key, you will have displayed

```
Message 1:
From martya Tue Nov 30 10:01:24 1993
From: martya@major.UUCP (Martin R. Arick ext 4892)
X-Mailer: SCO System V Mail (version 3.2)
To: martya
Subject: Good News
Date: Tue, 30 Nov 93 10:01:20 EST
Message-ID: <9311301001.aa05580@major.UUCP>
Status: R
hello from me
Marty
```

If you now wish to end the reading of your messages, you would enter the command

```
quit
```

and the following messages would appear

```
Saved 1 message in /u/martya/mbox
Held 0 messages in /usr/spool/mail/martya.
```

indicating that you had read all of the new messages and none were left in your mailbox. Any messages that you had not yet read will be saved for you to read later.

ADVANCED TIPS AND TECHNIQUES

Sending messages to others and reading messages from others form the heart of an electronic messaging system. As discussed earlier, the **mail** command provides these functions; but, there are two other messaging functions that are nice to have, though not essential: editing your message before mailing and saving messages that you have received. These two advanced functions are discussed here.

Editing Your Message before Mailing: Using the tilde Commands

After you enter the **mail** command with the names of the users to receive your mail, you will be placed in the input mode; every character that you type will be inserted into the message. Each line can be edited using the backspace key, but once the <Return> key has been pressed, the line can no longer be edited. When your message is complete, you can send it by pressing the Ctrl key and the D key together. But, suppose that you need to change the message before you send it. You can edit the entire message by using a **tilde** command to start up an editor. You can even use one of the **tilde** commands to insert a file into the message that you are creating. These **tilde** commands are subcommands of the **mail** command and are listed in Figure 8.1 with a short description of what each subcommand does.

As an example, suppose that you have issued the command

```
mail marick
```

and replied to the prompt

```
Subject: Bad News
```

and then entered the following lines of text to be in the message to send to *harry*

```
THis is not so good news.
Marty
```

At this point you decide that you need to change the message. You want to edit the message and at least indicate what the "Bad News" is. (You probably want to correct "THis" also.) To do that you would invoke the editor with the **tilde** subcommand

```
~v
```

Tilde Commands	What Tilde Command Does
~!shell-command	Executes shell-command and return
~.	Halts message input
~?	Prints a summary of tilde commands
~b name ...	Adds the *name(s)* to the blind carbon copy (bcc) list
~l^c name ...	Adds the *name(s)* to the carbon copy (cc) list
~d	Reads in the dead.letter file
~h	Prompts for "Subject" and "To", "cc", "bcc" lists
~M [msglist]	Inserts the specified messages into the letter, with no indentation
~m [msglist]	Inserts the specified messages into the letter, shifting the new text to the right one tab stop
~p	Prints the message being entered
~q	Quits from input mode by simulating an interrupt
~r filename	Reads in the specified file
~s string	Sets the subject line to *string*
~t name ...	Adds the *name(s)* to the "To" list
~v	Invokes a preferred screen editor on the partial message
~w filename	Writes the partial message onto *filename* file without the header

FIGURE 8.1 **Tilde** commands in input mode of **mail** command.

which will create a temporary file with your message in it and then start the **vi** editor to edit that message. Once you have the **vi** editor started, you can make any changes to the message that you wish. After you are finished, you will save the file with the usual **vi** command

```
zz
```

and you will get the messages

```
"/tmp/Re5589" 3 lines, 32 characters
(continue)
```

You can now add more to the message or mail it with the usual command pressing <Ctrl> and D keys together.

You can also create a message with a text editor (such as the vi editor) and pass it into the **mail** command as

```
mail harry < letter_to_harry
```

where the file, letter_to_harry, contains the message that you want to send *harry*. Creating the message before using the **mail** command to send it allows you to make sure that you have included all of the information that you wished and in the order in which you wanted to put it.

Keeping Your Messages: Saving Those Mail Messages

For any particular message there are several operations that you can perform which are summarized in Figure 8.2. The **mail** command is case-sensitive; thus, the command **f** means to save the message and the command **F** means to forward the message. The subcommand **s** will save the message to a file. The subcommand **d** will delete the message. Messages are numbered. You can refer to a message by its number. For example, if you wanted to save the message you had just read, you would enter the command

```
s 1 save
```

and the message

```
"save" [New file] 11/272
```

would be displayed indicating that the message was saved in the file named save.

The current message can be referred to by . (dot), while $ (dollar sign) is the last message and * (asterisk) is all messages. Most of the **mail** subcommands will operate on a list of messages. A range of message numbers can be specified by using a hyphen to designate a range of message numbers. Thus,

```
n-m
```

Mail Operation	Abbr	What Mail Operation Does
delete [msglist]	d	Deletes message from mailbox
forward [msgnum] user1	f	Forwards message to *user1*
respond [msgnum] user1		Responds to message with a message of your own
save [msgnum] filename	s	Saves message(s) in *filename*
type [msgnum]	t	Prints message on terminal
next	n	Displays next message
mail user		Sends a mail to *user*
quit	q	Quits, leaving messages unread
xit	e	Quits, saving messages
header	h	Displays list of active messages
top [msglist]		Displays first five lines of message
!		Executes shell command
list	l	Displays all commands
?		Displays explanations of commands

[msglist] is optional and specifies messages by number, author, and subject or type. The default is the current message.

FIGURE 8.2 Subcommands of the **mail** command.

is an inclusive list of messages from number n to number m.

Two **mail** operations of particular significance are f (forward the message) and r (reply to the message that has been received). When forwarding a message, you will be asked to provide the name of the person to whom you wish this message to be sent. When replying to a message, you will be placed in input mode so you can create your reply message. When you finish composing your reply, you will be asked if there are any people to receive this message by sending them a carbon copy (cc:).

You can save the message to a file using the **s** command. As part of the **s** command you would enter the name of the file in which to store the mail message.

PITFALLS TO AVOID

The worst problem that a mail system can have is its inability to deliver the messages. Problems with delivering messages are usually related to incorrect addressing of your message. Mail systems cannot deliver mail to someone whose address is close but is not quite correct. The *postmaster* of an electronic mail system is quite literal and generally will reject mail for people whose names do not match *exactly* any of the user names that the postmaster knows. These messages will be returned to the sender with the message "User unknown." Mail systems have the capability of providing aliases for users. If your name is easy to misspell, you might consider asking your postmaster to create an alias for you for the most obvious way that your name can be misspelled.

Mail systems are able to handle the problem of not being able to move the mail to the system to which the user is supposed to be connected. Mail systems will store mail that they cannot send to the proper system with the expectation that at some later time that system will be available to receive mail. However, these messages are stored only for a limited time, usually three days. If the target system is not available within this period, the mail will be returned to the sender.

PC CONSIDERATIONS

Personal computers have long had their own electronic messaging systems. These systems have usually been oriented toward their own local area networks. As networks have become more complicated, so have the needs of electronic messaging systems. Today electronic mail systems can receive the mail through various systems, including UNIX-based ones, DOS-based ones, and even VMS-based systems. These electronic mail systems can send messages to any known address on any type of system.

PC mail systems communicate with the **sendmail** server on various UNIX systems so that mail can be sent to users on UNIX systems or to retrieve mail that was sent by users that were on UNIX systems or just used the UNIX systems to move the mail from site to site.

PC mail systems have much better user interfaces than what the **mail** command provides. Function menus, lists of users' addresses, and group mailing lists are just a few of the abilities of the PC mail systems. For example, to compose a message, you operate in a window where you can edit your message as you create it. You can attach a file to your message with one touch of a menu option. You can send your message to any number of people whose addresses you have looked up by examining a pulldown list of known addresses.

INTERNET CONSIDERATIONS

Sending mail to another user on your system or within your network was discussed earlier in this chapter. The command that was invoked looked like

```
mail fred
```

But suppose you wanted to send mail to someone who wasn't on your system and isn't even registered as a user of your system. For an example, suppose you wanted to send mail to the user *fred* who is known to the system **remote.system.com** that is connected to the Internet, as illustrated in Figure 8.3. The **mail** command will handle this operation for you if you know the name of a system on which that user is known. To aid the **mail** command, you must add the name of the system to the name of the user as in

```
mail fred@remote.system.com
```

which would send the message to the system **remote. system.com** to be delivered to the user *fred*. Once you enter this command, the **mail** command will operate just as described in Chapter 11. As described earlier, the mail will be delivered even if the user is not currently on the system. The **mail** command does not care to whom you are sending the message.

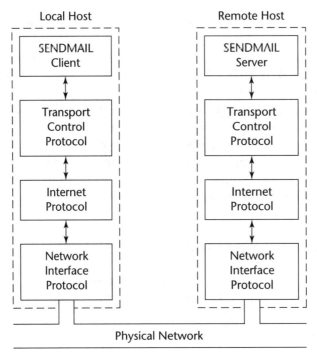

FIGURE 8.3 Sendmail interaction with protocols.

Furthermore, if you address your message incorrectly, the **mail** command will send it anyway. If the message proves to be unde-liverable, you will receive a message that will inform you of the failure.

For your message to be delivered to the intended user, some intermediate hosts will need to route your message from your system to the **remote.system.com** system. The routing sites in the Internet know about the systems that are connected to the Internet and, thus, can figure out how to send your message to that site.

The mail protocol services that the Internet provides are much the same as the mail services that are available in your own computer network. You even construct the message in the same way. The only difference is that the person to whom the message is addressed is located somewhere in the Internet and not in your local computer network. When someone who is not

on your system sends you a message, you can use the same **mail**
program to read that message.

The name of the system that you specify must be the name
that has been registered with the Internet organization and
known to other hosts in the Internet. The system's name within
the local network may be different. Once the message has been
delivered to the named system, the address can be changed to
an internal address which might not be known to the systems on
the Internet. Thus, in Figure 11.1 the system that is known as
goofy.mycmpny.com to the Internet may be known as just
goofy within the local network.

BEHIND THE SCENES

The **sendmail** server moves messages (that is to say, mail) from
one host to another with the goal being to move the message to
the host on which the user resides. To assist **sendmail** in this
noble task, aliases are defined which inform the **sendmail**
server which users are defined on this host. Other messages
received by the **sendmail** server will be moved onto another
host that can deliver the message to the intended user.

The **sendmail** server can be queried to determine whether
it knows the address of the users that are defined on the remote
host. To check out how various users are defined, a user connects to the **sendmail** server and queries it to determine which
users the **sendmail** server knows about. Users can connect to
the **sendmail** server by using the **telnet** command to attach to
the remote host of interest with the well-known port of the
sendmail server. For example, if the user enters the command

```
telnet ranch.company.com 25
```

the **sendmail** server will respond:

```
Trying...
Connected to ranch.company.com.
Escape character is '^]'.
220 ranch.company.com 5.65c/IDA-1.4.4 Sendmail is ready
    at Mon, 14 Sep 1992 21:37:26 -0400
```

Once the connection to the **sendmail** server is established, the requesting host should identify itself as in the following:

```
helo Local.Company.com
```

The **sendmail** server will acknowledge the requesting host with the reply

250 Hello Local.Company.com, pleased to meet you

If the user incorrectly identifies the local host, the **sendmail** server will respond

250 Hello Local.What.com why do you call yourself Local?

The following command can be used to query whether the **sendmail** server knows about a particular user:

```
vrfy marty
```

The **sendmail** server will respond with the full name of the user asked about if the user's name is known or the message "550 marty ... User unknown" if the user is not known.

If you want to know what commands were defined, enter the **help** command; the reply would be:

```
214-Commands:
214-   HELO   MAIL   RCPT   DATA   RSET
214-   NOOP   QUIT   HELP   VRFY   EXPN
214-For more info use "HELP <topic>".
214-To report bugs in the implementation contact
     sendmail@okeeffe.Berkeley.EDU
214-For local information contact postmaster at this site.
214 End of HELP info
```

If you want to determine the contents of a mailing list, use the **expn** command. If the mailing list exists, the **sendmail** server will respond with the names of the users on that mailing list.

SMTP defines a set of commands with strict syntax that are used to move mail messages from one host to another. These functions are not user-visible. To set up mail systems requiring addresses of users, there is usually another command on the system; for AIX it would be sendmail. The **sendmail** command will set up aliases and mail addresses so that mail can be sent from one user to another.

SMTP delivers mail by establishing a transmission path between an SMTP client (in the literature, this is called a Sender-SMTP) and an **SMTP** server on a remote host (in the literature, this is called a Receiver-SMTP). Once this pathway is established, the SMTP client sends a message to the **SMTP** server indicating who the recipient of the mail is (using an SMTP RCPT command). If the SMTP server can accept mail addressed to that user, it will reply with an OK; if it cannot, it will reject that recipient. This type of negotiation will proceed for several recipients until the SMTP client has exhausted its list of recipients for which it has mail.

Once the list of recipients has been agreed upon, the SMTP client transmits the mail messages to the **SMTP** server (using **mail** commands).

SMTP has been implemented in a manner that is independent of the transport protocol used. For TCP/IP-based networks, TCP is used as the transport mechanism, as illustrated in Figure 8.3. Some hosts provide the service of delivering mail directly to a user's terminal. SMTP provides compatibility with this method of operation by defining commands which implement "sending." Delivery of mail to a mailbox is considered to be "mailing." To support this, the various forms of the **send** command replace the **mail** command in the interaction between the SMTP client and **SMTP** server.

SUMMARY

The **mail** command is usually described in a manual page on your UNIX system. In addition, there are several mail reading programs, some commercially available, which provide a number of services to make the reading and writing of mail messages easier. These will usually be described in their own manual pages.

The protocol for a mail services server is described in RFC 821 called "Simple Mail Transfer Protocol" written by Jonathan B. Postel, August, 1982. A companion text, "Standard for the Format of ARPA Internet Text Messages" (RFC 822), describes how message addresses should be formatted so that mail servers can understand them and can deliver the mail properly.

mount Command

INTRODUCTION

Files that physically reside on a remote host can seem to be locally available in the sense that local operations can be performed on them, such as editing or using them in a program that is executing on the local host. Making remote files locally available is effected by using Network File Services to create Network File Systems. The original work in this area was done by Sun Microsystems Incorporated. Currently, these services are not a part of the standard TCP/IP suite, but there are a number of proposals to standardize the network file services and add them to the TCP/IP protocol suite. This chapter will describe what the network file services can do and how this is accomplished.

GETTING STARTED WITH NETWORK FILE SYSTEMS

Earlier chapters described moving files from a remote host onto a local host so that these files can be accessed on the local host. Each of these methods involved making a copy of the file on the local host. Network file systems allow access to files on remote

115

hosts from a local host without copying the files onto the local host. These remote files behave just like local files.

To make remote files available on a host requires that the file systems themselves on the remote host be made available on the local host. Executing the **mount** command creates a local directory that is a place-holder for the remote directory on the remote host. The **mount** command will make even local file systems available. The **mount** command does not require that the user know whether the file system is local or remote, if an appropriate entry for the file system is found in the /etc/filesystems file. The **mount** command does not require that the user start a user session on the remote host. The command

```
mount /happy/large
```

will request that the file system **/happy/large** be made available to users on this host. The entry in the /etc/filesystems file informs the **mount** command that this file system is located on the host **happy** and the file system on that remote system is called **/large**. Once the **mount** command finishes, a user can examine any file in the **/happy/large** file system in much the same way they examine or use a file in a local file system.

Part of the entry in the /etc/filesystems file provides information to the **mount** command on which host this file system is located. Once the **mount** command is successful, the distinction between local file systems and remote file systems will not be visible.

For file systems that are not registered in the /etc/filesystems file, the **mount** command must contain the information about where the file system is physically located. Thus, the **mount** command

```
mount ranch:/goodstuff /ranch/goodstuff
```

is a request to mount a directory on **ranch** called **/goodstuff** as **/ranch/goodstuff**. Usually, remote file systems are mounted on a local system using the name of the host and the name of the remote file system. A remote file system can be mounted on a local system under a name different from its name on the remote system, but users can be confused by this approach. Once a file system is successfully mounted, changing to the **/ranch/goodstuff** directory on the local system will make available to the local user the same files that a user on that remote system sees.

A user can determine if a file system is on the local host or on the remote host by using the **df** command or by examining the permissions attributes of a file in that file system. The **df** command is simply

```
df /happy/large
```

which requests information about the directory **/happy/large**. The information may look like

```
Filesystem     Total KB   used       free      %used    Mounted on
happy:/large   1247180    1077308    169872    86%      /happy/large
```

which indicates that the directory **/happy/large** is actually on a remote host named **happy**. If the user executes the command

```
ls -l /happy
```

the display would be

```
Drwxrwxrwx 32 root adm 1024 Sep 17 18:01 large/
```

If the user executes the command

```
ls -l /happy/large
```

the display would be

```
Frw-r-----   1 marty   adm      7600    Sep 10 15:26 acaca.prtx
Drwxr-xr-x   2 marty   adm       512    Jul 07 16:02 about/
Frwxr-xr-x   1 marty   adm      9922    Aug 31 16:50 backup.out*
Drwxr-xr-x   2 marty   adm       512    Aug 18 17:31 config/
Drwxr-xr-x   2 marty   adm       512    Jul 09 16:12 convert/
Frwxr-xr-x   2 marty   adm      4434    Sep 11 16:12 commit*
Frw-r-----   1 marty   adm     13927    Aug 31 14:21 database
```

Filesystem	Total KB	used	free	%used	Mounted on
/dev/hd4	53248	42388	10860	79%	/
/dev/hd2	253952	249224	4728	98%	/usr
/dev/hd9var	4096	1980	2116	48%	/var
/dev/hd3	8192	1188	7004	14%	/tmp
jerico:/usr/local	262144	232752	29392	88%	/usr/local
jerico:/u	49152	44280	4872	90%	/u
happy:/large	1247180	1077308	169872	86%	/happy/large
goofy:/usr/local2	81548	63572	17976	77%	/usr/local2
sleepy:/good	524280	33744	490536	6%	/good

FIGURE 9.1   Sample output from **df** command.

where the capital letters, "F" to designate a file and "D" to designate a directory, indicate these are remotely located files and directories. Unfortunately, not every version of UNIX marks remote files this way; some versions do not change the type on a remote file.

To obtain a list of the file systems currently available on a host, the user would use the **df** command. As an example, a display of the various file systems on a particular host is displayed in Figure 9.1. For this system there were two file systems from the host **jerico** plus one system each from the hosts **happy**, **goofy**, and **sleepy**. (The file systems called **/dev/hdX** are local file systems.) Note that it is not necessary for the directory name on the remote host to be the same as the directory name on the local host. For practical reasons, system administrators generally include the name of the remote host in the name by which the local host knows that file system.

 ADVANCED TIPS AND TECHNIQUES

The **mount** command can be used to indicate what file systems are currently available on this host by issuing the **mount** command without any arguments as in

```
mount
```

The output from this command might look like

```
Node    Mounted        vfs     Options
jerico /usr/local     nfs     bg,soft
happy  /happy/large  nfs     bg,soft
```

which indicates that there are two remote file systems mounted, one from the remote host **jerico** and the other from **happy**.

You can mount one file system over another. The file system underneath will no longer be available. Instead, any access to that file system will be mapped to the file system on the remote host. If you unmount the remote file system, the contents of the local file system will be made available.

For most systems, both local and remote file systems can be described in a special file called filesystems which is usually in the /etc directory. Each entry in this file will describe a file system indicating its location, name of directory in that location, and the name of the directory by which it is to be known on the local host. Chapter 12 has more information on the contents of /etc/filesystems. Some sample entries from such a file are shown in Figure 9.2 which describes the **/usr/local**, **/happy/large**, and the **/usr/local2** remote file systems.

Once the file system has been made available on the local host by use of the **mount** command, operations on that file system are exactly the same as for a local file system. The hosts do not enforce any extra security on accessing the file system. Further, the local user does not start a user session on the remote host. Thus, NFS can be used to make available a file system from a host on which the user has no access rights. The access rules for the remote file system mounted on a host are the same as those for a local file system. The system administrator can limit the type of access that a user on the local host will have through the usual UNIX system commands.

 PITFALLS TO AVOID

When a system is not available, the files on that system are not available. Part of network file services is to make the real location of a particular file invisible to the user. The user will not

```
/usr/local:
    dev                 = /usr/local
    vfs                 = nfs
    nodename            = jerico
    mount               = true
    check               = false
    type                = nfs
    options             = bg,rsize=1024,wsize=1024
/happy/large:
    dev                 = /large
    vfs                 = nfs
    nodename            = happy
    mount               = true
    check               = false
    type                = nfs
    options             = bg,hard,intr,rsize=1024,wsize=1024
/usr/local2:
    dev                 = /usr/local2
    vfs                 = nfs
    nodename            = goofy
    mount               = true
    check               = false
    type                = nfs
    options             = bg,hard,intr,rsize=1024,wsize=1024
```

FIGURE 9.2   Sample entries in /etc/filesystems file.

normally know that files are not local to a host because the network file services operate behind the scenes to provide data from a file without notifying the user that the file is not located on the local host.

If you try to access a remote file and that file is no longer available, your command will not fail; instead, your command will not complete. No command-line prompt will reappear. Your process appears to be "hung" and doesn't complete. If you are able to interrupt the process with a Ctrl-Z character, you will be able to "kill" the process to stop it and a command-line prompt will appear. Because NFS does not maintain a connection to the remote host, it does not know that the host is no longer available; therefore, it is not able to notify the user that there is a problem. Only when NFS tries to access the file will it learn that the host is no longer operating properly. As is discussed later in this chapter, NFS relies on sending a command to the remote host to retrieve a block of data from a file or to write a block of data into a remote file. But no permanent connection between the local host and the remote host exists. Thus, the local host does not know the state of remote operations on the remote host.

PC CONSIDERATIONS

The ability to have PC files visible to UNIX systems has been implemented extensively. Usually, the goal is to show a file system on the UNIX host that is physically on a PC. These mounted PC file systems operate just like remote UNIX file systems. Since they are really DOS file systems, the naming conventions of the DOS systems have to be maintained. Unfortunately, long directory names and long filenames are truncated.

Some implementations of NFS for UNIX hosts will enable the mounting of file systems from PC network servers. These file systems can appear to be just like UNIX file systems, even if physically they are on PCs. Since NFS is a relatively simple protocol, a number of implementations on various platforms have been made.

INTERNET CONSIDERATIONS

Network file services are not currently available on the Internet. If you want access to a particular file on a remote host, you will have to copy that file to the local host using **ftp** or you will have to start a user session on that remote host.

BEHIND THE SCENES

Network file services are requested from the remote host using Remote Procedure Calls (RPCs). As illustrated in Figure 9.3, the RPC mechanism allows individual commands to be sent to the remote host to be performed on that remote host, much like the **rsh** command. These commands are executed and the results are returned to the originating host. Figure 9.4 lists the various NFS commands that can be executed and the type of information that will be returned.

Commands executed using an RPC pathway are synchronous. That is to say, the requestor will wait for the reply from the **RPC** server before continuing to execute the requestor's program further. The reply from the **RPC** server contains all of the information that was requested. The requestor does not acknowledge receipt of the information; no further messages need to be executed.

All filename processing is performed on the remote system itself so that the local system does not need to know very much about the remote file system. The only expectation that the local system has is that the remote file system is hierarchical. The pathname is parsed by the client so that differing pathnaming conventions can be managed. The pathnames are examined one component of the path at a time.

NFS is stateless. NFS does not keep records of which record in a file was accessed or even which file was accessed. Any state information such as file- or record-locking must be implemented as a separate service since NFS contains no such services. When the requested operation completes successfully, data must have been read or written even if the server crashes along the way.

FIGURE 9.3 Remote procedure calls (RPCs).

Network File Services Command	Description
Get File Attributes	Gets attributes of a file on a remote system
Set File Attributes	Changes the attributes of a file on a remote system
Look Up File Name	Gets pointer to file on remote system
Read from Symbolic Link	Gets symbolic link for file on remote system
Read from File	Reads data from file on remote system
Write to File	Writes data to file on remote system
Create File	Creates a file on remote file system
Remove File	Deletes a file on remote system
Rename File	Renames a file on remote system
Create Link to File	Creates a hard link to a file on the remote file system
Create Symbolic Link	Creates a symbolic link to a file on the remote file system
Create Directory	Creates a directory on remote file system
Remove Directory	Deletes a directory on remote file system
Read from Directory	Reads directory entries from remote file system
Get Filesystem Attributes	Gets attributes of remote file system

FIGURE 9.4 Network file services commands

SUMMARY

This chapter has described how file systems on remote hosts can be made available on local hosts without copying any files using network file system functions.

Manual pages describe the **mount** command and the **df** command. Three RFCs form the basic documentation of how the Network File Services operate: RFC 1094 describes the overall approach to Network File Systems; RFC 1050 describes the Remote Procedure Calls that are used by the Network File Services clients and servers; RFC 1014 describes how data that is managed by the Network File Services is encoded.

Miscellaneous Network Services

INTRODUCTION

A number of services may be offered as part of a TCP/IP-based network. These services are optional but, if they are offered, they must follow a defined standard protocol. Several of these services are useful in diagnosing network problems. These optional services are listed in Figure 10.1. Each of these services is described in this chapter.

Each of the various miscellaneous network services is used by establishing a connection to a remote host using the **telnet** command with the appropriate TCP port number for that service as discussed in Chapter 3. The TCP port number assigned to each of these services is shown in Figure 10.1 as well as a brief description of the service. A system does not have to implement any of these services but, if it does, that system must use the assigned port number for that service.

ECHO NETWORK SERVICE

The echo service will send back to the originating application any data it receives. The echo service can operate as either a

Network Service	Port	What Service Does
Echo Service	7	Sends back to requester any transmitted message
Discard Service	9	Discards all messages that it receives
Active Users Service	11	Sends back to requester which users are active on remote system
Daytime Service	13	Sends back to requester the date and time including day of the week, month of the year
Character Generator Service	19	Sends back to requester all of the possible printable ASCII characters
Time Service	37	Sends back to requester time in seconds since midnight January 1, 1900

FIGURE 10.1 Miscellaneous TCP/IP network services.

connection-based TCP service or a connectionless UDP service. As a connection service, the **echo** server listens on TCP port 7 for TCP connection requests. Once the connection is established, any data that is received is sent back to the originating application. The echoing of messages will continue until the connection is broken. An **echo** server also listens on UDP port 7 for datagrams. When a datagram is received, the data in it is sent back to the originating source. Since the data that is received is just sent back to the originating application, the performance of the network could be tested by measuring the time that it takes for the data to arrive at the remote host and be transmitted back. This turnaround time will measure the response time and latency in the network connection between the host and the remote host to which it is connected.

As an example, you can invoke the echo service on the host **rodeo** with the command

```
telnet rodeo 7
```

which will establish a connection to the echo service of **rodeo** (if it is running). Such a telnet session might look like the following (you enter the lines in bold):

```
Trying...
 Connected to rodeo.company.com.
 Escape character is '^T'.
sssss<return>
sssss
ssssssss<return>
ssssssss
jjkkll<return>
jjkkll
^T
```

Notice that when you type in any characters and touch the Return key, those characters will be echoed back to you on your terminal. The message that will be echoed is only sent to the echo server when you press the Enter key. Also notice that the echo service will continue to respond to you until you press Ctrl+T keys which halts the telnet session and breaks the connection with the remote host.

DISCARD NETWORK SERVICE

The discard service discards any data that is sent to it. It operates both as a TCP connection-based service and as a UDP-based connectionless service. As a TCP service, a server will listen at the TCP port 9 for connections; when a connection is established, it will discard any data sent to it without reporting an error or sending back a response. As a UDP service, a server will listen at the UDP port 9 for datagrams and will discard any datagrams it receives without any error and without sending a response.

To invoke the discard service, you would enter the command

```
telnet rodeo 9
```

The same date as used previously to show how the echo service behaves would look like

```
Trying...
 Connected to rodeo.company.com.
 Escape character is '^T'.
sssss<return>
ssssssss<return>
jjkkll<return>
^T
```

where no response is received from the remote host **rodeo** but no error is signaled either and the connection is continued for as long as is wished.

ACTIVE USERS NETWORK SERVICE

The active users service will send back to the originating source a list of the users currently active on the host. The TCP active users service listens at port 11. When a connection is established it will respond with a list of the currently active users and then will close the connection. The UDP active users service listens at UDP port 11; when a datagram is received, it will respond with a list of users.

For example, you can issue the command

```
telnet ftp.uwp.edu 11
```

which requests that the host **ftp.uwp.edu** send you a list of the currently active users with the name of the port on which they logged in, when they logged in, and from what system they logged in. Such a reply might look like

```
Trying...
 Connected to cs.uwp.edu.
 Escape character is '^]'.
 hfagher    ttyp3    Dec  8 07:19    (gordo.uwp.edu)
 triad      ttyp4    Dec 15 16:25    (wilco.uwp.edu)
 wilson     ttyp6    Dec  7 17:06    (grass.uwp.edu)
 jjones     ttyp7    Dec 15 21:00    (good.uwp.edu)
 gorden     ttyp8    Dec 15 22:08    (good2.uwp.edu)
 winston    ttyp9    Dec 14 08:51    (harris.uwp.edu)
```

which indicates that six users were active on the system at the time this command was run. Not all systems implement this service. This type of information can be useful if you are searching for a system on which to work that is not heavily loaded.

DAYTIME NETWORK SERVICE

The daytime service sends back to the originating source the date and time in the format: day of the week, month of the year, day of the month, time in HH:MM:SS, and the year. Each of these fields will be separated by blanks. The TCP daytime service listens at TCP port 13. When a connection is established, it will respond with the date and time, and then close the connection. The UDP daytime service listens at UDP port 13. When a datagram is received, it will respond with the date and time as the remote host knows it.

For example, the command

```
telnet snoopy 13
```

will establish a connection to the daytime service on host **snoopy**. The output from that command will be displayed on your terminal and will look like

```
Trying...
Connected to snoopy.companyname.com.
Escape character is '^T'.
Connection closed.9 1995
```

which indicates that a standard telnet connection is established long enough for the date and time to be sent from the remote host **snoopy** and then the connection is closed. This type of command could be used to determine the date and time on a set of computers in a network and ensure that they all have the same date and time. The time of a second host was checked using the command

```
telnet grumpy 13
```

and its time was Wed Mar 15 19:58:09 1995 which indicates that one of the two hosts needs to have its time adjusted.

CHARACTER GENERATOR NETWORK SERVICE

The character generator service simply sends character data of a proscribed format to any source that connects to it or sends a datagram to the character generator service. Any input that is sent to it will be ignored. The TCP character generator service listens at TCP port 19 for TCP connection. Once a connection is established, the input is discarded and a stream of character data in a particular pattern is sent to the originating source. Data will continue to be sent until the connection is broken. Users may abort the connection at any time. The normal TCP data flow mechanism will keep the character generating process from sending the user data faster than it can process it.

The UDP character generator service listens for datagrams on UDP port 19. When a datagram is received, a datagram is sent to the originating source which contains a random number (between 0 and 512) of characters. One popular pattern for sending the character data is a 72-character line of ASCII characters, generated from the 95 printable ASCII characters. Such a pattern is illustrated in Figure 10.2. The set of 72 characters that is sent is rotated so that eventually all 95 ASCII characters have been sent. Thus, you can test the ability of a printer to print all the ASCII characters and the ability of the network to transmit properly all 95 ASCII characters.

As another example, the command

```
telnet rodeo 19
```

will establish a connection to the character generator service on host **rodeo**. This connection will cause a stream of characters, such as is shown in Figure 10.2, to be displayed on your terminal until you abort the connection with the Ctrl+T keys. This service can be used to test your terminal and determine if there are any common ASCII characters that cannot be displayed by your terminal.

```
!"#$%&'()*+,-./0123456789:;<=>?@ABCDEFGHIJKLMNOPQRSTUVWXYZ[\]^_`abcdefg
!"#$%&'()*+,-./0123456789:;<=>?@ABCDEFGHIJKLMNOPQRSTUVWXYZ[\]^_`abcdefgh
"#$%&'()*+,-./0123456789:;<=>?@ABCDEFGHIJKLMNOPQRSTUVWXYZ[\]^_`abcdefghi
#$%&'()*+,-./0123456789:;<=>?@ABCDEFGHIJKLMNOPQRSTUVWXYZ[\]^_`abcdefghij
$%&'()*+,-./0123456789:;<=>?@ABCDEFGHIJKLMNOPQRSTUVWXYZ[\]^_`abcdefghijk
%&'()*+,-./0123456789:;<=>?@ABCDEFGHIJKLMNOPQRSTUVWXYZ[\]^_`abcdefghijkl
&'()*+,-./0123456789:;<=>?@ABCDEFGHIJKLMNOPQRSTUVWXYZ[\]^_`abcdefghijklm
'()*+,-./0123456789:;<=>?@ABCDEFGHIJKLMNOPQRSTUVWXYZ[\]^_`abcdefghijklmn
()*+,-./0123456789:;<=>?@ABCDEFGHIJKLMNOPQRSTUVWXYZ[\]^_`abcdefghijklmno
)*+,-./0123456789:;<=>?@ABCDEFGHIJKLMNOPQRSTUVWXYZ[\]^_`abcdefghijklmnop
*+,-./0123456789:;<=>?@ABCDEFGHIJKLMNOPQRSTUVWXYZ[\]^_`abcdefghijklmnopq
+,-./0123456789:;<=>?@ABCDEFGHIJKLMNOPQRSTUVWXYZ[\]^_`abcdefghijklmnopqr
,-./0123456789:;<=>?@ABCDEFGHIJKLMNOPQRSTUVWXYZ[\]^_`abcdefghijklmnopqrs
-./0123456789:;<=>?@ABCDEFGHIJKLMNOPQRSTUVWXYZ[\]^_`abcdefghijklmnopqrst
./0123456789:;<=>?@ABCDEFGHIJKLMNOPQRSTUVWXYZ[\]^_`abcdefghijklmnopqrstu
/0123456789:;<=>?@ABCDEFGHIJKLMNOPQRSTUVWXYZ[\]^_`abcdefghijklmnopqrstuv
0123456789:;<=>?@ABCDEFGHIJKLMNOPQRSTUVWXYZ[\]^_`abcdefghijklmnopqrstuvw
123456789:;<=>?@ABCDEFGHIJKLMNOPQRSTUVWXYZ[\]^_`abcdefghijklmnopqrstuvwx
23456789:;<=>?@ABCDEFGHIJKLMNOPQRSTUVWXYZ[\]^_`abcdefghijklmnopqrstuvwxy
3456789:;<=>?@ABCDEFGHIJKLMNOPQRSTUVWXYZ[\]^_`abcdefghijklmnopqrstuvwxyz
456789:;<=>?@ABCDEFGHIJKLMNOPQRSTUVWXYZ[\]^_`abcdefghijklmnopqrstuvwxyz{
56789:;<=>?@ABCDEFGHIJKLMNOPQRSTUVWXYZ[\]^_`abcdefghijklmnopqrstuvwxyz{|
6789:;<=>?@ABCDEFGHIJKLMNOPQRSTUVWXYZ[\]^_`abcdefghijklmnopqrstuvwxyz{|}
789:;<=>?@ABCDEFGHIJKLMNOPQRSTUVWXYZ[\]^_`abcdefghijklmnopqrstuvwxyz{|}~
```

FIGURE 10.2   Output from character generator network service.

TIME NETWORK SERVICE

The time service sends back to the originating source the time in seconds since midnight January 1, 1900. This type of service is used to synchronize time on a set of hosts. The TCP time service listens at TCP port 37. When a connection is established, it will send the current time and then close the connection. The UDP time service listens at UDP port 37. When a datagram is received, it will respond with the current time as a 32-bit binary number.

For example, the command

```
telnet rodeo 37
```

will establish a connection to the time network generator service on host **rodeo**. The output from that connection would look something like

```
Trying...
    Connected to rodeo.company.com.
    Escape character is '^]'.
    ....Connection closed.
```

which indicates that the connection to **rodeo.company.com** was made and the time service replied with four characters that were not printable and are shown as "....". These four bytes are the time in a 4-byte binary format which is in seconds. For example, one value received from a host was b3120c26 and another was b3120b99 which shows that the time between these two hosts differs by 135 seconds or about 2 minutes and 15 seconds. This is a significant difference and indicates that you should change the time on one of the hosts.

Network Service	RFC
Echo Service	862
Discard Service	863
Character Generator Service	864
Quote of the Day service	865
Time Service	868
Daytime Service	867
Active Users Service	866

FIGURE 10.3 RFCs describing miscellaneous network services

SUMMARY

A variety of miscellaneous network services can be available for use as network test tools or to enable a standard date and time on every host throughout the network. One service will echo back to the source host any data it is sent. Another service will send to the requesting host output that contains all of the printable ASCII characters. Another service will return to the requesting host a list of users currently active on that host.

Each of the miscellaneous network services is described in a separate RFC. Figure 10.3 lists the RFC which is the basis for each of the services. For further study of any of these services, users can examine the appropriate RFC.

11

Special Internet Commands

OVERVIEW

As discussed in earlier chapters, TCP/IP is found on all UNIX hosts and many non-UNIX hosts as well. The wide availability of a common standard communications protocol led to the establishment of institution-wide networks using TCP/IP to provide easy access to information within a company. Since many institutional networks were using a common protocol, exchanging information *between institutions* became possible and a network that allowed communications between institutions could be created. Thus, the Internet was born.

The first part of this chapter discusses what the Internet is and what services are offered on the Internet. Earlier chapters examined three of the four basic Internet functions: electronic mail (Chapter 8), file transfer between computers (Chapter 7), and remote login to another computer (Chapter 2). The fourth basic function, Usenet newsgroups, will be discussed here. Finally, Internet browsers are discussed.

WHAT IS THE INTERNET?

The Internet is a worldwide network of computer networks communicating with each other using the TCP/IP protocol.

Every network site on the Internet has a unique name and address assigned by an Internet organizing body called the Merit Network Information Center which coordinates the assignment of names and addresses so that each name and address will be unique. The Internet can be viewed as one large network where the distinguishable parts are the systems whose names are known and the rest of the network is just there to provide connectivity to the systems of interest. Figure 11.1 illustrates that view by showing all of the Internet as a "cloud" of computer systems with the known target systems themselves connected to this cloud. In Figure 11.1 the local site is **goofy.mycmpny.com** and the remote sites (actual Internet site names) are **wuarchive.wustl.edu**, **gatekeeper.dec.com**, and **town.hall.org**.

Names of systems in the Internet usually have from two to four levels as shown in Figure 11.1, each separated by a period (.). Single-level names such as "mars" or "jupiter" would not be unique enough for a large network. The lowest level usually identifies what kind of a site it is or what foreign country it is in. For example, a company's Internet name will end in .com, a government institution in .gov, an educational institution in .edu, an organization in .org, an Australian site in .au, an English site in .uk, and so on. Thus, in Figure 11.1, **wuarchive.wustl.edu** is a university (Washington University in St. Louis), **gatekeeper. dec.com** is a company (Digital Equipment Corporation), and

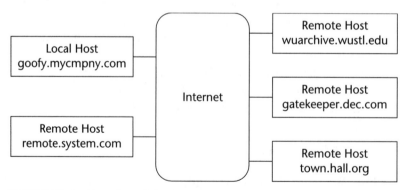

FIGURE 11.1 One view of the Internet.

town.hall.org is an organization. One famous government Internet site is **whitehouse.gov**.

Certain sites are designated as routing sites so that messages can be sent through the network from one site to another, even if these two sites were not in the same network. Information about where in the network individual sites are located is sent around the Internet to all of the routing sites, so that when a message for a particular site arrives at a routing site, that site will know where next to send the message.

The Internet provides four services to its users: electronic mail, Usenet newsgroups, file transfer between computers, and remote login to another computer. In order to use any of these services (except for electronic mail) you must first be connected into a local host which has access to the Internet. Each of these services can be invoked from the command line using a serial connection. Thus, even using modems and a phone line as a serial connection to log into a host that has access to the Internet enables all of these functions. This type of account is sometimes called a *shell* account because you are operating under the control of a shell program when you are logged into a system. Some newer internet-browsing software that provides a graphical view of the Internet and has menus of functions and automates the searching of Internet sites for information and the transfer of files requires a network connection to the Internet. Usually, this is done with a network interface board, but special dial-up connections can provide a network connection using modems; these connections are called Serial Line Interface Protocol (SLIP) connections. How these operate is beyond the scope of this book.

GETTING STARTED WITH THE INTERNET

Part of the function of the Internet is for users to exchange information. Two users sending mail to each other are exchanging messages, but only the two users that exchanged the messages will get to read them. More information could be exchanged if there was some way people could send messages that would be distributed to many Internet sites. The Internet society solved this problem by creating a conferencing system that organizes the information around a set of *newsgroups* which cover a very wide range of topics of interest.

Reading the news groups is quite simple; just execute one of the news reader commands as in

```
trn
```

and you will receive a response like

```
Unread news in ne.food              23 articles
Unread news in ne.forsale          121 articles
Unread news in comp.archives         4 articles
Unread news in comp.dcom.servers    29 articles
Unread news in comp.misc           113 articles
```

```
etc.
====== 23 unread articles in ne.food -- read now? [+ynq]
```

The news reader keeps a list of which news groups each user is interested in and summarizes what "articles" each user has not read in each news group. An *article* is a message that someone has sent to this news group. An extensive set of help messages will lead you through the techniques of reading and subscribing to news groups. You can choose to read a news group or skip that group until later.

You inform the Internet in which news groups you are interested by "subscribing" to that news group and reading the messages that others have sent to that news group. News groups covering any computer topic are available. This type of conferencing is similar to sending messages to mailing lists of users who have expressed interest in some set of ideas.

Once you choose to read a news group, you will be provided with a list of the articles that you have not read and their titles as in

```
comp.dcom.servers 28  articles
a Robert Mah          2    Experiences using LANs...
  shai@pixel.co.il
b Brian J. Smith      1    >Terminal servers ...
```

```
d mick@woodstock.g     1    >Best Server/router?
e Me@telematrix.co      3    New Telecom Resource ...
  Leonard Conn
  C Hollenbaugh
f Barbara Gavin         1    Client\Server Seminars: ...
g Steve Morytko         2    Authentication for ...
  Carl Rigney
i Brad                  2    Vendors FAQ
  Wolfgang Henke
j Alwin Mulder          1    On Demand servers
l Rudi van Drunen       1    Annex routing
o Benjamin BROCHET      1    Avis a tous les ...
r Bill Neal             1    Slipping on Citrix?
s James Taylor          2    Net Access With TV ...
  John Holmes
t Elazar                1    Where can I find DEC's ...
Select threads (date order) -- Top 67% [>Z] --
```

where the author of the article is shown at the left and the title
of the article is shown at the right. The news reader organizes
the messages into *threads* which are messages that relate to
each other. The number of the messages in any thread is the
number shown between the author and the title. You can choose
any of these threads to read by pressing the letter at the far left
for the messages of interest or skip to the next page of messages
by pressing the space key on your terminal.

Newsgroups cover many different interests from a wide
range of computer topics to music to art to food, and so on. New
newsgroups can be easily formed when new topics of interest are
discovered. A few of the newsgroups to which you might sub-
scribe are listed in Figure 11.2. This figure gives a very small
selection of the newsgroups which number in the thousands.

When users want to contribute their ideas about a topic of
interest, they send a message, not to a particular user, but to the
newsgroup that has that topic as its focus. This operation is
called *posting news* and uses a command called **Pnews**. Once a
message has been posted to the news group, everyone who reads
that news group will receive that message. Anyone can post a
message or a question to a news group; there are no special
qualifications to contribute to any particular news group.

Newsgroup	Discussion Topic
comp.archives	Software available via Anonymous ftp
comp.unix.aix	General IBM AIX
comp.unix.hp	General HP UNIX
comp.unix.questions	General UNIX questions
comp.unix.shell	UNIX shell programming
comp.unix.wizards	UNIX internals, system administration
comp.answers	Answers to Frequently Asked Questions (FAQ)
comp.dcom.servers	Data communications servers TCP/IP discussions
news.announce.conferences	Announcement of conferences
news.announce.newsgroups	Announcement of new newsgroups
comp.org.ieee	IEEE Discussions
rec.music	General music interests
comp.music	Computer music
ne.food	Restaurants in New England
ne.forsale	Items for sale in New England

FIGURE 11.2   Some Usenet newsgroups available on the Internet.

Many news groups gather the answers to the most frequently asked questions in a document known as the Frequently Asked Questions (FAQ) list which is posted to the news group on a monthly basis. One archive site, **rtfm.mit.edu**, serves as a repository site for these documents.

Messages from the various news groups of interest are gathered by one of your local computer systems by accessing a network news server and downloading messages of interest. Individual users inform their own news server in which news groups they are interested and the local news server will interrogate the remote news server for the list of new messages and new groups. Only messages that the user wants to read are actually downloaded to the news reader's system.

ADVANCED TIPS AND TECHNIQUES

All of the services previously described can be used from the command line, but do not provide a user-friendly interface. Once connected to a remote site using **ftp**, neither a menu of available files nor a guide to what information is stored there is presented to the user. To remedy this user interface problem, Internet *browsers* were developed; they have a graphical face and provide menus of functions and items to choose from. One of the earliest of these browsers is called Mosaic and is publicly available from **ftp.ncsa.uiuc.edu**. An Internet browser requires a TCP/IP connection to the Internet.

The Internet browser takes advantage of a special kind of Internet server called a **WorldWide Web** (**WWW**) server. **WWW** servers provide search functions through the use of hypertext. **WWW** servers have special addresses called uniform resource locators (URL). To examine the contents of a **WWW** server, you start your Internet browser and inform your browser of the URL of the **WWW** server of interest. The browser then queries the server and retrieves a list of resources that are available at that server or that the server knows about. This information is presented to the user as documents with keywords that can be chosen to retrieve new information. A few **WWW** servers to look at are listed in Figure 11.3.

PC CONSIDERATIONS

As discussed in earlier chapters, most of the Internet services have been implemented on the personal computer (PC). Using electronic mail on the PC was described in Chapter 8. Transferring files between your site and an Internet site was discussed in Chapter 7. Logging into an Internet site was discussed in Chapter 3.

Internet browsers have also been implemented for the PC. Using these services from a PC is much like using these services from a UNIX host. The system must be directly connected to the network and able to access the Internet on its own. Internet

WWW Server	WWW Server Contents
http://www.census.gov	Census bureau
http://www.whitehouse.gov	White House documents to browse
http://sunsite.unc.edu	FAQ browser
http://www.tig.com/IBC/index.html	Internet business
http://www.eren.doe.gov	Department of Energy
http://www.ksc.nasa.gov	Kennedy Space Center
http://www.uniforum.org	Uniforum '95
http://www.digital.com	Music
http://icweb.loc.gov/ homepage/ichp.htm	Library of Congress
http://cad.ucla.edu/ repository/usefule.tarot.html	Tarot card reading

FIGURE 11.3 Some WorldWide Web sites.

browsers for the PC are available from a number of sources on the Internet itself via file transfer. Several commercial implementations are now on the market which promise more functionality, such as menuing front ends or printing various reports.

SUMMARY

This chapter introduced the Internet and the services that it provides: electronic mail, Usenet newsgroups, file transfer between computers, and remote login to another computer. Examples of how to use the Usenet newsgroups were given. Examples of the information that is available to be transferred from other computers was listed.

A wide range of books that concentrate just on the Internet is available from bookstores. These books will have lists of important and useful Internet sites. In addition, many newspapers offer a weekly column reviewing interesting Internet sites.

A Guide to TCP/IP Files

INTRODUCTION

Earlier chapters described how various TCP/IP applications provide various functions for users in a networked environment. Chapters 15 through 18 will describe how the various protocols in the TCP/IP protocol suite cooperate to move data from one application on one host to a second application on a second host. Some parts of this software need information to operate effectively; this information is organized in a series of files. This chapter will focus on the TCP/IP files.

Part of the administration of a TCP/IP network is to manage the contents of a number of files that control the TCP/IP network functions. Each of the files has a specific purpose and needs to be maintained if all of the various functions of a TCP/IP-based network are to work properly.

THE HOSTS FILE

Nodes in a network are registered in a file called /etc/hosts. Any node named in this file can be sent messages if its name is known. Nodes that are not in this file can still be sent messages, but only if their internet address is known or a name server is

127.0.0.1	localhost		
192.129.16.11	snoopy	linus	gertrude
192.129.16.12	farm	sleepy	
192.129.16.13	ranch	corral	

FIGURE 12.1   Contents of a typical /etc/hosts file.

running. A typical /etc/hosts file is shown in Figure 12.1. Each entry in the file shows: (1) the internet address and (2) at least one name for that node on the network. Multiple names can be specified for any computer on the network. The first name listed is usually thought of as the name of the node; the other names are called *alias names*. Any alias names for the host can be included by being entered on the same line as the internet address for that node. This file is used to translate the name of a host into an internet address.

Examining the typical /etc/hosts file shown in Figure 12.1, the host named "snoopy" has the internet address of 192.129.16.11 and two alias names of "linus" and "gertrude." The internet address and name of the local host must be in this file because the local host will use the contents of the /etc/hosts file to determine its own internet address. The address 127.0.0.1 is a special address reserved for testing the local network software.

THE EQUIVALENT HOSTS (*hosts.equiv*) FILE

The hosts.equiv file in the /etc directory lists the names of hosts that are permitted to execute certain remote commands such as **rsh**, **rcp**, and so on, on the local host without supplying a password. (For a description of what each of these commands do, see the appropriate chapter in this book.) This file is often called the *equivalent hosts* file because each of the hosts in this file can perform many of the same commands that the local host can perform. In addition, the same user name must be defined on the remote host as the user name on the local host, although the

snoopy

farm

ranch

groucho

harpo

FIGURE 12.2 Contents of a typical /etc/hosts.equiv file.

passwords can be different. Some implementations do not allow the user name to be the "root." The **rlogind** server, **rshd** server, and **lpd** server check the /etc/hosts.equiv file before executing the requested command. Each entry in the /etc/hosts.equiv file, as illustrated in Figure 12.2, consists of the name of the host that is permitted to execute commands on the local host. This host name must also be in the /etc/hosts file. As many names of hosts can be listed as desired. They are listed one name to a line.

THE REMOTE HOSTS (*.rhosts*) FILE

The .rhosts file specifies the names of remote users who are not required to supply a login password when they execute the **rcp**, **rlogin**, and **rsh** commands using a local user's account when the remote user and the local user are not the same. This file is placed in the local user's Home directory as specified in the /etc/passwd file. This file must be owned by the local user and its permissions must restrict access to the local user only. The existence of this file allows access to one's files from remote hosts; thus, this file should be created and populated carefully. If the ownership and the permissions on the file are not set correctly, most implementations of TCP/IP servers will ignore this file and refuse access to a remote user.

A sample .rhosts file, as shown in Figure 12.3, contains entries that list the name of the remote host and the name of the user on that remote host who is requesting access to the

snoopy	sam
farm	jerry
groucho	fred
harpo	samantha

FIGURE 12.3 Contents of a typical .rhosts file.

local user's files. Each pair of names, remote host and remote user, must be on separate lines and must be separated by blanks or tabs.

If the sample .rhosts file were in the Home directory of *sally* and owned by *sally* and had permissions of "600" (read/write only by owner), then the user named *sam* from the host **snoopy** or the user named *jerry* from the host **farm** could log in to *sally*'s account without specifying a password.

THE *.netrc* FILE

The .netrc file provides information used by the **tftp** and **ftp** commands to automatically connect to a host without requesting either a user name or a password. This file must be placed in a user's Home directory (as specified by the environment variable HOME or as specified in the /etc/passwd file), must be owned by the user, and must have access permissions that permit reading by the owner only. If you do not fulfill this last condition, the **ftp** command will assume that this is not a valid file and will not use entries in it.

A sample .netrc file is shown in Figure 12.4. The file contains the keyword "machine" and the name of the host, the keyword "login" and the name of the user, and the keyword "password" and the password of the user separated by spaces, tabs, or new lines. The keywords must be included as shown, but entries can be on several lines.

When the **ftp** command or the **rexec** command executes, the .netrc file in the Home directory of the user on the local host

| machine snoopy | login sam | password goodtimes |
| machine farm | login jerry | password jerrypass |

FIGURE 12.4   Contents of a typical .netrc file.

is read to be able to supply the user name and password that is valid on the remote host. Thus, the example in Figure 12.4 specifies that when the remote user logs into **snoopy** as user named *sam*, the password to specify is *goodtimes*.

THE */etc/services* FILE

The /etc/services file specifies the port number and protocol used by a particular application. This file is used by the various servers to determine what port to listen at for requests for the particular service that the server provides. Figure 12.5 illustrates a typical /etc/services file. For user-written applications that will use TCP/IP services and need to use a port to listen at or to send messages from, it is a good idea to add entries to the /etc/services file so that other servers can make sure that they do not use ports that are being used by other applications. Port numbers less than 1,024 are reserved for system applications.

An operating system call can be used to find the port number for a particular application on the local host. Port numbers for various TCP/IP services are assigned by a central agency (Internet Application Board) so that any other service that wishes to communicate with one of those TCP/IP services on a remote host will know what port number to use. These ports are called *well-known* port numbers. Services can be added and port numbers assigned to them but these port numbers must not use any of the well-known and previously assigned port numbers.

Each entry in the /etc/services file consists of the official internet service name, the port number used for that service, which transport layer protocol is used, and any unofficial names (aliases) that service might be known by. For example, in the example file, the **ftp** server uses port 21 for communications and uses TCP as its transport protocol.

echo	7/udp		
discard	9/udp	sink null	
systat	11/tcp		
daytime	13/tcp		
netstat	15/tcp		
ftp	21/tcp		
telnet	23/tcp		
smtp	25/tcp	mail	
time	37/tcp	timserver	
name	42/tcp	nameserver	
whois	43/tcp		
mtp	57/tcp		# deprecated
nicname	101/tcp	hostname	# usually from sri-nic
#			
# Host specific functions			
#			
tftp	69/udp		
rje	77/tcp		
finger	79/tcp		
link	87/tcp	ttylink	
supdup	95/tcp		
pop	109/tcp		# Post Office Protocol
#			
# UNIX specific services			
#			
uucp	251/tcp		# MASSCOMP specific
exec	512/tcp		
login	513/tcp		
shell	514/tcp	cmd	# no passwords used
courier	530/tcp	rcp	# experimental
biff	512/udp	comsat	
who	513/udp	whod	
syslog	514/udp		
talk	517/udp		
route	520/udp	router routed	# 521 also
timed	525/udp	timeserver	

FIGURE 12.5 Contents of a typical /etc/services file.

THE */etc/filesystems* **FILE**

The /etc/filesystems file defines a set of the file systems on this host. The **mount** command uses the entries in this file to determine how to make the file system available to the local users. Such file systems can be local, that is to say, physically on this host, or remote, that is, physically on some other host. Each entry in this file is composed of several lines—starting with the name of the file system—that are usually called a *stanza*. Each succeeding line in a stanza starts with one of the keywords listed in Figure 12.6.

Keyword	Meaning of Keyword
account	Whether accounting system will process this file system
check	Whether to check file system with fsck, usually check local file system but not remote file system
dev	Identifies file or directory to be mounted; for local mounts give name of block special file
mount	Set to "automatic" to cause file system to be mounted when system is started; set to "true" if this file system is managed by the mount command; set to "false" to keep the mount command from managing this file system
nodename	Gives name of remote host that contains this file system
options	Set to "bg" if nfs mount is to be performed in the background; set to "fg" if nfs mount is to be performed in foreground; set to "rsize=xxxx" to specify the size of the read buffer as xxxx; set to "wsize=yyyy" to specify the size of the write buffer as yyyy; set to "hard" so that the request will be retried until server responds; set to "soft" so that server not responding will be reported as error; set to "retry=z" to limit number of attempts to mount file system to "z"; set to "intr" to allow keyboard interrupts during mount attempts
type	Used to group related mounts
vfs	Specifies type of mount; "nfs" indicates this is mounted as an nfs file system; "bootfs" indicates this is local file system
vol	Specifies label for volume when initializing

FIGURE 12.6   Keywords in /etc/filesystems file.

/happy/large:	
dev	= /large
vfs	= nfs
nodename	= happy
mount	= true
check	= false
type	= nfs
options	= bg,hard,intr,rsize=1024,wsize=1024

FIGURE 12.7   Sample entry in /etc/filesystems file.

The *nodename* and *dev* values for a file system indicate on which host the file system is and what its name is on the remote host. The *options* keyword specifies what action to take if the request to mount a remote file system is not successful or if access to the file system fails. Multiple values are possible for this keyword. For example, one possible value for the *options* keyword specifies how many retries to make to mount the file system and whether this process will halt until the mount is successful. Another value for this keyword determines the size of the read and write buffers. Any of the *options* entries can be specified on the command line when you execute the **mount** command.

A sample entry in the /etc/filesystems file is shown in Figure 12.7 which describes the network file system **/happy/large** which is the file system **/large** on the remote host **happy**. This file system is to be mounted "hard" as a background command and to allow interrupts from the keyword.

THE PASSWORD FILE

The passwd file in the /etc directory contains the names and passwords of all the users that are authorized to access this particular host. Most network commands will fail if the user in whose name the command is executed is not defined on the remote host. The password that a user has on different hosts need not be the same. The password can be specified in the /etc/passwd file but may not be, for security reasons.

In addition, the /etc/passwd file contains several other important pieces of information. The various fields that each entry in the /etc/passwd file contains is shown in Figure 12.8. Each field is separated from the others by a colon (:). A typical entry in the /etc/passwd file is shown in Figure 12.9.

The Home directory listed in the /etc/passwd file for a particular user is the directory that the user will be placed in when logging in from a remote host. This directory can be local to this host or one that is located on another host in your network. Once you have started a user session on a host, the name of your Home directory is in the environment variable HOME. The shell name identifies the program that is started for you when you log in. All your interactions with the host will be through this program. Any program can be specified, but usually this program is one of the shell programs: **/bin/ksh** for the Korn shell, **/bin/sh** for the Born shell, or **/bin/csh** for the C shell. Each of these shells has differing capabilities and, worse, different command

Field Name	Meaning of Field
User Name	Login name of user
Password	Encrypted password for this user or exclamation point ("!") if password stored somewhere else
User id	Numeric string, usually uniquely identifying the user; to be used in attaching ownership to files
Group id	ID of group that user belongs to
User Information	Miscellaneous string, usually identifying user; often user's full name
Home Directory	Full pathname of directory in which user will be placed when session starts; usually directory that contains user's files
Shell Name	Name of shell program to start when user logs in

FIGURE 12.8   Fields in the /etc/passwd file.

```
martya:!:234:78:Marty Arick:/jerico/home/martya:/bin/csh
```

FIGURE 12.9   Sample entry in /etc/passwd file.

syntax. A discussion of the shell programs is beyond the scope of this book.

The user id denotes the number that will be assigned as the owner of any file that this user creates and the group id is the number of the group to which this user belongs. The ownership of a file is shown as a name of a user in displays that the **ls** command produces. The matching of user id with user name is done by scanning the /etc/passwd file and examining the user id entries.

SUMMARY

This chapter has concentrated on reviewing the contents and purpose of the various files that are used by the TCP/IP software. The hosts file identifies the various hosts in the network while the equivalent hosts file (hosts.equiv) identifies remote hosts whose users can perform the same commands on the local host as the local users. The .rhosts file specifies remote users who are permitted to operate in the Home directory of a local user without specifying the local user's password. The .netrc file specifies users and remote hosts that can connect to the local host without specifying a password. The password contains the information that describes a user of the local system. The services file specifies the port number that a particular remote TCP/IP service uses.

Network Security and Troubleshooting

INTRODUCTION

Earlier chapters have discussed the role of the system administrator in creating user accounts on a UNIX system. Networks need to have their own administrator because two particular network-related areas need managing: network security and troubleshooting. Because networks are being interconnected via the Internet, network security is an important issue. The network administrators must manage access to their own networks or unwelcome outsiders will access their systems. The first part of this chapter is devoted to a discussion of some of the issues surrounding security in a network.

A second concern of the network administrator must be the performance of the network. As more and more systems are added to the network, the traffic on the network will increase and performance will be an issue. The second part of this chapter will examine network performance.

SECURITY IN TCP/IP NETWORKS

Allowing access to your hosts for only the users that you intended is the goal of security in a TCP/IP network. As discussed previously, once a user is logged into a system, the security within that system is all that prevents the user from accessing information that user should not be able to access. Thus, the first level of security in a network is to make sure that all the security on the various hosts themselves is carefully policed. Unfortunately, security in UNIX hosts is based on user id and password. Thus, user ids and passwords need to be very difficult to guess. The most effective method used to create a truly secure system is to have user ids that are not personal names or initials but computer-generated in some reasonably random style and to have passwords that are likewise computer-generated. Users will not like having user ids and passwords that are not easy to remember. But, if someone trespassed into your system, that person will be able to work out user ids if it appears that some form of a person's name is being used as a user id. If you find using computer-generated user ids too difficult, you should at least force people to change their passwords regularly. Further, you should regularly use password scanning software to make sure people aren't using simple, easy-to-guess passwords like their birthday or car type.

A second level of security is to ensure that only users who you want are even accessing your network. If your network is completely disconnected from the outside world, you only need to concentrate on the security of your individual hosts. But if you are part of the Internet community and have linked up to the outside world, you need to consider measures to isolate your network from the rest of the Internet. One method is to place a "wall" between your network and the outside networks. This mechanism is often called a *firewall* because a "fire" in the outside network will not be allowed to enter your network. As shown in Chapter 14, routers can be programmed to analyze the network address of a user attempting to access your network and exclude those addresses that are allowed. Thus, routers can be used as firewalls to filter out the network addresses of users who you do not want to access your system.

One other issue of security: The **rlogin** command is sometimes used in place of the **telnet** command because system administrators can set up user validation so that no password is needed for a user to log in on another host. The **telnet** command always requires a password to be entered. Unfortunately, this approach, while convenient for users, opens a security hole on the remote system when you use it. With access to the outside world via the Internet a reality for many networks, you should not have any passwordless user ids. If you need to provide a *guest* password for a short period of time, you should create a special account for this purpose and then only assign a password when you want to provide access to that guest. By the way, user ids on most UNIX systems can be set up not to allow login on that user id at all. These user ids are normally present in the system for allowing ownership of system files.

Another issue of security involves permitting the use of anonymous file transfers. Chapter 7 reviews how this is done. You can set up your system so that a file can be transferred between your system and another system without the user having a user id registered on your system. This is accomplished by setting up the ftp user with a special Home directory for that user. Then a user can log in using the user anonymous and any password will be accepted for that user. Once logged in, the anonymous user will have access to those files that are in the Home directory of the anonymous user. With careful attention to the permissions on other directories, only this one directory can be made available to outside users.

TESTING NETWORK CONNECTIONS

As part of the network layer providing message routing from one host to another, TCP/IP provides one protocol (the Internet Protocol) to move packets from one host to another and a second to support the determination of the physical path through the network from one host to another called Internet Control Message Protocol (ICMP). One of the services that ICMP performs is *echo responding*—when a node receives an ECHO_RESPONSE message from another host, it is required to send an acknowledgment back to that host. Thus, if you wanted to determine whether a node was connected to a network and responding, another node could send an ICMP message to that node and expect a response. If no response was received in a reasonable period of time, it would be assumed that node was not on the network.

The command that sends the ECHO_RESPONSE message to another host is called the **ping** command. (Some have claimed that the name of this command is short for Packet Internet Groper.) This command is usually found in the /etc directory with other system-oriented commands. The simplest form of this command

```
ping host1
```

would send messages to the host **host1** and measure how long it takes for the reply to be received. This process will be repeated for as long as is desired. If no response is received, the command will hang and not return. Each receipt of a message is usually accompanied by output which indicates how long the round trip to the remote node was. Receiving responses from a remote node is proof that the remote node is connected and properly defined on the local host. Usually, the **ping** command will indicate what internet address it is using for that remote host. It is possible to use an internet address in place of the name of the host if the particular host of interest is not yet defined on the local system.

The **ping** command has several options that can be used to examine the performance of your network. By default the packet size that **ping** uses is 64 bytes. A different packet size can be specified on the command line such as

```
ping host1 1024
```

which would send packets of 1,024 bytes to the remote host named **host1**. The time that this size packet takes to make the round trip to the remote host is a measure of how the network is performing. It is also possible to specify how many times to send the message to the remote host, such as

```
ping host1 1024 25
```

which would send packets of 1,024 bytes to the remote host named **host1** 25 times and then stop and print a summary of the timings.

Finally, it is possible to use the **ping** command to determine pathways through a network by specifying the -o option on the command. Thus, the command

```
ping -o host1
```

would list the intermediate internet hosts that were traversed in getting the message from the local host to the remote host.

EXAMINING NETWORK PERFORMANCE

The performance of the network can be analyzed by using a variety of techniques, the most basic of which is the **netstat** command. The **netstat** provides several different sets of output depending on which option is chosen. The **netstat** command will display different types of information about the various parts of the network setup.

For example, the performance of the network interface hardware can be examined by using the **-v** option on the **netstat** command. Figure 13.1 shows the output from **netstat -v**.

The memory that is allocated to the network routines can be examined by using the **netstat -m** command as illustrated in Figure 13.2.

The state of the current connections between hosts can be displayed by using the **netstat -n** command as shown in Figure 13.3. In this display the port number of the application on each host is attached to the internet address of that host with the type of protocol being used shown to the left of each entry. "ESTAB" indicates that the connection is established.

The current state of the routing tables is displayed by the **netstat -r** command, while statistics about the various protocols are shown with the **netstat -s** command. The statistics for the TCP protocol are shown in Figure 13.4 and the statistics for the ICMP protocol are shown in Figure 13.5.

The command **netstat -i** will show the state of the various hardware interfaces and **netstat -id** will show the state of the interfaces with the count of dropped packets as illustrated in Figure 13.6.

ETHERNET STATISTICS (en0) :
Hardware Address: 02:60:8c:2e:09:04

Transmit Byte Count: 18134446	Receive Byte Count: 6520501
Transmit Frame Count: 43757	Receive Frame Count: 57285
Transmit Error Count: 0	Receive Error Count: 0
Max Netid's in use: 7	Max Transmits queued: 1
Max Receives queued: 0	Max Stat Blks queued: 0
Interrupts lost: 0	WDT Interrupts lost: 0
Timeout Ints lost: 0	Status lost: 0
Receive Packets Lost: 0	No Mbuf Errors: 0
No Mbuf Extension Errors: 0	Receive Int Count: 57285
Transmit Int Count: 43757	CRC Error Count: 0
Align Error Count: 0	Recv Overrun Count: 0
Packets Too Short: 0	Packets Too Long: 0
No Resources Count: 0	Recv Pkts Discarded: 1172
Xmit Max Collisions: 0	Xmit Carrier Lost: 0
Xmit Underrun Count: 0	Xmit CTS Lost Count: 0
Xmit Timeouts: 0	Parity Errors: 0
Diag Overflow Count: 0	Execute Q Overflows: 0
Execute Cmd Errors: 0	Host side End of List Bit: 0
Adpt side End of List Bit: 0	Adapter pkts to be uploaded: 57285
Adapter pkts uploaded: 57285	Start receptions to adpt: 1
Receive DMA timeouts (lock up): 0	

FIGURE 13.1 Output from **netstat -v** command for Ethernet.

158/384 mbufs in use:
    1 mbufs allocated to data
    4 mbufs allocated to packet headers
    59 mbufs allocated to socket structures
    84 mbufs allocated to protocol control blocks
    2 mbufs allocated to routing table entries
    6 mbufs allocated to socket names and addresses
    2 mbufs allocated to interface addresses
0/46 mapped pages in use
232 Kbytes allocated to network (8% in use)
0 requests for memory denied

FIGURE 13.2 Output from **netstat -m** command.

Active Internet connections					
Proto col	Recv Queue	Send Queue	Local Address	Foreign Address	(state)
tcp	0	0	130.151.158.148.513	130.151.156.103.1020	ESTAB
tcp	0	0	130.151.158.148.1026	130.151.156.59.6000	ESTAB
tcp	0	0	130.151.158.148.1025	130.151.156.59.6000	ESTAB

FIGURE 13.3 Output from **netstat -n** command.

tcp:
    14307 packets sent
        13251 data packets (9654670 bytes)
        0 data packets (0 bytes) retransmitted
        992 ack-only packets (927 delayed)
        0 URG only packets
        6 window probe packets
        9 window update packets
        49 control packets
    13894 packets received
        4535 acks (for 2927337 bytes)
        24 duplicate acks
        0 acks for unsent data
        3089 packets (94703 bytes) received in-sequence
        0 completely duplicate packets (0 bytes)
        0 packets with some dup. data (0 bytes duped)
        28 out-of-order packets (798 bytes)
        0 packets (0 bytes) of data after window
        0 window probes
        194 window update packets
        0 packets received after close
        0 discarded for bad checksums
        0 discarded for bad header offset fields
        0 discarded because packet too short
    18 connection requests
    17 connection accepts
    35 connections established (including accepts)
    38 connections closed (including 2 drops)
    1 embryonic connection dropped
    9795 segments updated rtt (of 1 attempts)
    1 retransmit timeout
        0 connections dropped by rexmit timeout
    0 persist timeouts
    0 keepalive timeouts
        0 keepalive probes sent
        0 connections dropped by keepalive

FIGURE 13.4 Output from **netstat -s** for TCP protocol.

```
icmp:
        17 calls to icmp_error
        0 errors not generated 'cuz old message was icmp
        Output histogram:
                destination unreachable: 12
        0 messages with bad code fields
        0 messages < minimum length
        0 bad checksums
        0 messages with bad length
        Input histogram:
                echo reply: 3
                destination unreachable: 32
                source quench: 2
                routing redirect: 2
                time exceeded: 3
        0 message responses generated
```

FIGURE 13.5 Output from **netstat -s** for ICMP protocol.

Name	Mtu	Network	Address	Ipkts	Ierrs	Opkts	Oerrs	Coll	Drp
lo0	1536	<Link>		342	0	342	0	0	0
lo0	1536	127	localhost	342	0	342	0	0	0
en0	1500	<Link>		679020	0	581046	0	0	0
en0	1500	168.238.11	test.host.com	679020	0	581046	0	0	0
et0	1492	<Link>		23391	0	10131	0	0	0
et0	1492	none	none	23391	0	10131	0	0	0

FIGURE 13.6 Output from **netstat -id** command.

What all these numbers will show you is whether this particular system sees a network that is overloaded or whether the network interface card on this system is overloaded. If you sense a problem in your network, the main approach you can take is to create subnetworks and place a router between them. Chapter 14 discusses how a router works and how it can filter out messages. Thus, a router could lower the traffic on segments of your network. Figure 13.7 shows a network with four hosts. Without

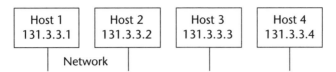

FIGURE 13.7 Network with four hosts.

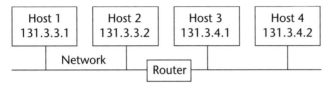

FIGURE 13.8 Subnetted network with four hosts.

routers any message going from one host to another will be received and analyzed by every host on the network. If the network was split into two sections with a router in between, as shown in Figure 13.8, messages that are going from the host with the address 131.3.3.1 to host 131.3.3.2 need not be seen by every host on the network. Usually, subnets are created (Chapter 16 discusses subnets) and the router is programmed to analyze to which subnet the message is directed. In Figure 13.8, two subnets have been set up: 131.3.3 and 131.3.4. Thus, messages that originate in subnet 131.3.3 and are directed to another host in that subnet would not be retransmitted onto subnet 131.3.4.

SUMMARY

For further information, you can examine the manual pages that describe the files that have been discussed in this chapter. The manual pages for the **ping** command and the **netstat** command review many other options for the commands that were not discussed in this chapter.

The OSI Model of Communications Networks

INTRODUCTION

In this chapter a widely discussed model of communications networks is examined. This model, although not strictly adhered to by TCP/IP, provides a framework for the discussion of the inner workings of TCP/IP in the chapters that follow. An understanding of the model will enable us to understand why TCP/IP is constructed the way it is.

WHAT IS THE OSI MODEL OF COMMUNICATIONS NETWORKS

An interconnected set of lines and terminals allowing processing to take place in one or several locations is usually viewed as a network. A network may have several hosts interacting with multiples of terminals. To bring structure to this view of a network, the concept of network architecture is proposed; this is a structured hardware and software design that supports the interconnection of a number of physical and logical components.

A network architecture is a way to define the set of rules to which these interconnecting elements must conform. It is not, however, a definition of how the internal design is made or how the functions in the network operate or how a rule is actually implemented. A network architecture is a statement of what services need to be provided to enable the network to follow one set of rules.

In the past several years the International Organization for Standardization (ISO) has developed a model of network architecture called the Open Systems Interconnection (OSI) model of network architecture. The goal of this model is to promote the interconnecting of networks of all types.

The underlying principle exploited by the OSI model is *layering*. The idea is to create a network architecture with several layers where each layer provides certain unique functions which are not provided by any of the other layers, and the interface between each layer is strictly defined. Based on some standard structuring techniques, the OSI model defines seven distinct layers, as shown in Figure 14.1. Each layer need only interact with the adjacent layers and has no knowledge about any other layers, as illustrated in Figure 14.2. Information flows down through the layers of the sending host and then up through the layers of the receiving host. Because the layers are isolated from each other by strict interfaces, information that is added by a layer in the sending host will only be used by the matching layer in the receiving host. In this sense the matching layers of the sending and receiving hosts communicate with each other in a peer-to-peer relationship, as illustrated by the dotted lines connecting matching layers in Figure 14.2.

Each layer adds value to the services provided by the set of lower layers in such a manner that the highest layer is offered the set of services needed to run an application distributed over several networks. Each layer provides services to the layer above and requests services from the layer below. Thus, the total network problem is divided into a set of smaller problems.

Intermediate networks that merely relay information from one network to another will only need to implement some of the lower three layers to act as transferal agents. Figures 14.3, 14.4, 14.5, and 14.6 illustrate this principle of the OSI scheme for differing network problems.

7. Application	Layer
6. Presentation	Layer
5. Session	Layer
4. Transport	Layer
3. Network	Layer
2. Data Link	Layer
1. Physical	Layer

FIGURE 14.1 Seven layers of the OSI model communications network.

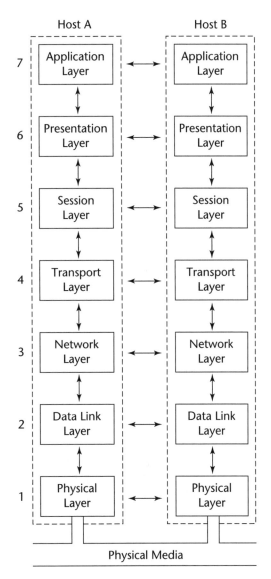

FIGURE 14.2 How OSI model hosts communicate on the same network.

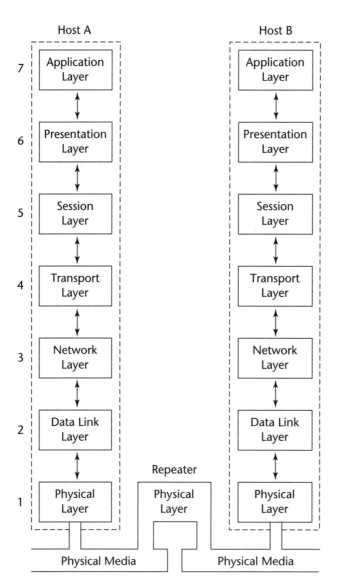

FIGURE 14.3 How OSI model hosts communicate through repeaters.

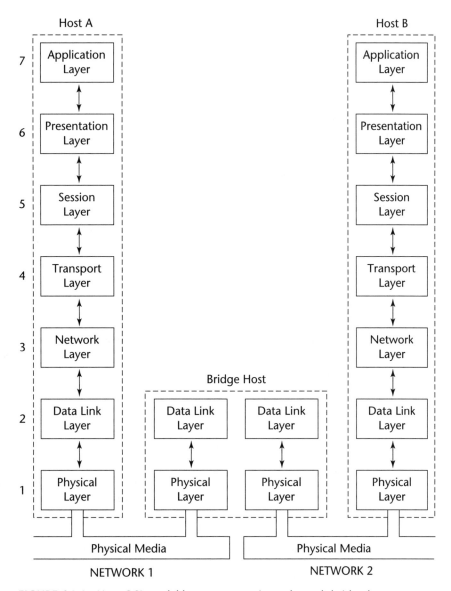

FIGURE 14.4 How OSI model hosts communicate through bridge hosts.

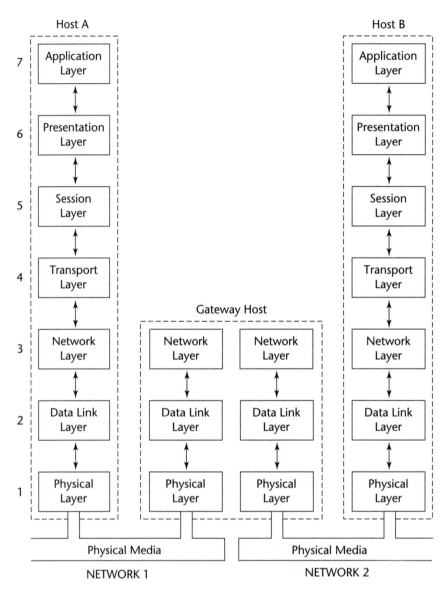

FIGURE 14.5 How OSI model hosts communicate through gateway.

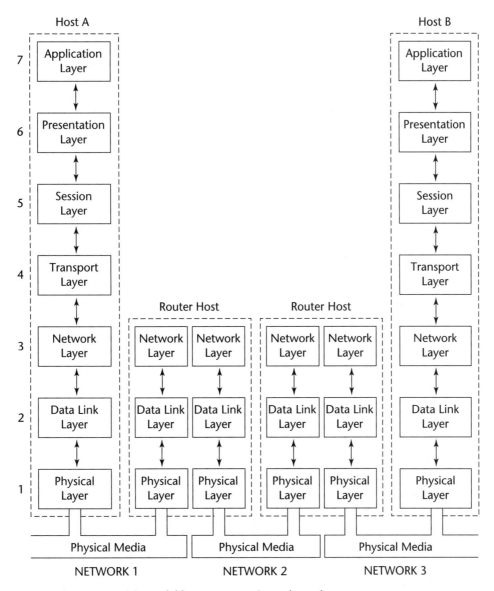

FIGURE 14.6   How OSI model hosts communicate through routers.

THE SEVEN LAYERS IN THE OSI MODEL

Each of the layers has a different unique set of functions to perform. Layer 1, the physical layer, provides the mechanical, electrical, and procedural characteristics to establish, maintain, and release physical connections between data-link entities. This layer provides the physical link between devices and the network. Some of the current standards in this layer are RS-232-C and RS-449. This layer sends and receives a stream of bits across the medium, providing a physical connection between two communicating systems.

Layer 2, the data-link layer, provides the functional and procedural means to establish, maintain, and release data links between network entities. This layer ensures that transfers of data take place error-free on noisy channels and provides error correction and sequencing. All of these functions will probably require extra information to be added to the data. Some methods add to the end of the message a checksum (on which all of the bits in the message have been calculated) which is used to test whether this message was correctly received. This layer will cause retransmission of the message if there is an error. Some of the current definitions of this layer include Ethernet, Token Ring, and so forth.

Layer 3, the network layer, provides for the exchange of information between two entities over network connections. This layer allows node-to-node type of operations in a network where intermediate systems (hosts) may be used only for moving data around. This layer is a delivery service; layers above this one will not be able to transfer information from one physical node to another physical node. This layer provides independence from routing and switching considerations for the rest of the network. It controls routing between nodes with no direct connection by querying intermediate nodes to determine a route between non-physically connected hosts. Thus, intermediate nodes need only contain up to the network layer in order to provide message relay services.

Layer 4, the transport layer, is for the transparent transfer of data between session entities (processes) that need not worry about data transfer between each other in a cost efficient manner. This layer is needed so that the available communications service can be optimized to provide network performance needed at a minimum cost. It segments messages into smaller pieces if the lower layers cannot handle the full message at one time or if it were more cost effective to do so. The transport layer implements flow control so that lower layers are not swamped with data.

Layer 5, the session layer, binds and unbinds distributed activities into relationships. Binding is the setting up of communications between two processes and includes sending from one process to the other any necessary parameters that describe the originating process. This layer controls data exchange, synchronizes data operations between two entities, and controls the dialogue between two users. The session layer determines the way data is sent, either in one direction only, in both directions alternatively, or in both directions at the same time. It structures the dialogue between the two communicating systems.

Layer 6, the presentation layer, handles the representation and manipulation of data for the benefit of the application programs. This layer handles the transformation of terminal data from the "real" terminal device or application data generator into a standard terminal data stream by performing code and format translation. This *virtual terminal* concept represents all terminal functions in a standard way. In this model, the network knows only one type of terminal, the virtual terminal. Message compression and/or encryption can be done in this layer.

Layer 7, the application layer, is the highest layer and handles the management of the OSI network. This layer is responsible for collecting data concerning the establishment of connections for data transfer between application processes. It provides different services depending on what the application needs. Not much work has been done on this layer where information processing occurs.

The OSI model forms the framework that all current and future networks will be measured against. Further, there is wide agreement that the OSI model is a needed development; therefore, manufacturers of data communications equipment and software will work to conform to the OSI model.

When two hosts are located in the same network, this layering methodology may seen cumbersome and not necessarily providing functionality. Figure 14.2 illustrates this case of two hosts on the same network. Notice the flow of data down the different layers and then back up the different layers. The next section will examine situations that require applying these techniques in order for data to move from one host to another. For example, how do you move data from one host in one network that uses one set of protocols to a host on another network that uses an entirely different set of protocols?

APPLYING THE OSI MODEL TO TWO COMMUNICATING HOSTS

The OSI Model predicts three different possibilities exist for enabling communications between two hosts: (1) connection through the physical layer, (2) connection through the data-link layer, and (3) connection through the network layer. Which possibility is chosen will depend on the services that each of the two communicating hosts needs. Each of these three cases will be analyzed in the following discussion.

Suppose that the physical location of two hosts extends beyond the limitation of the physical layer characteristics (more than 1,500 meters for Ethernet-based data-link layers with coaxial cable). How can you then move messages from Host A to Host B? Because of the layering methodology only the contents of the physical layer would need to be moved from Network 1 to Network 2. Figure 14.3 illustrates interconnecting two hosts on different networks through a device that operates only at the physical layer level. This device need only copy the electrical signals from one network to the other and vice versa. These devices are called *relays* or *repeaters*.

Repeaters are physical-level devices that just copy electrical signals from one segment of a network to another. Repeaters are often used in local area networks (LANs) to extend the network. Ethernet-based local area networks have a limited range based on the time it takes for a signal to travel to the end of the cable and back again. This length is roughly 1,500 meters. If all of the network devices cannot be co-located within this distance, the network can be extended by inserting a repeater to resend the signal from one network to the other.

The second case is that the two networks are compatible down to the data-link layer. For this type of interconnection a device that operates at the data-link level will be needed. Such a device, called a *bridge*, is illustrated in Figure 14.4. This illustrates the case of one network that uses Token Ring as its data-link layer and the other network that uses Ethernet as its data-link layer.

Bridges connect two networks logically and will copy messages from one network to another. Bridges operate at the data-link layer. They often contain logic so that messages (frames) that are not bound for a host on the other network are not passed to that network. Bridges need to be configured with the addresses of devices that are on each of the networks that it is connecting. Usually, bridges operate on physical addresses but some can operate on Internet addresses.

Bridges connect local area network segments that are too large to be constructed as one. They forward packets from one network segment to another until the segments reach the local area network that contains the host that is being addressed. In a network with a number of separate local area networks tied together packets may travel through a number of bridges before finding the correct local area network. Bridges operate at the data-link layer and base their filtering and forwarding decisions on the hardware address of the network interface cards. As such, they are geared to handle the protocol and addressing scheme of a particular type of data-link layer.

The third case is that the two networks are compatible only down to the network layer. In this case two different devices exist: gateways and routers.

Gateways are devices that interconnect two or more networks. They often perform some specific protocol conversion at layers above the network layer to move data from one type of network to another as shown in Figure 14.5. For example, suppose two different networks want to exchange data; one network is based on Digital Equipment Corporation's DECNET protocol and the other is based on TCP/IP protocol. A gateway can be used to move data from one network to the other. A gateway has network connections in each of the different networks that you want to connect together and its job will be to take messages from one network and move them to the other network, performing whatever protocol translations are necessary.

Routers operate at the network layer and move messages that are bound for a node that is on a network that is distant from the current network to a network that is connected to the network that the node is on, as shown in Figure 14.6. Routers make logical decisions about the pathway through the networks and usually operate on the addresses that the particular protocol provides.

Routers can be used to create a barrier between a local network and the outside world. That is to say, all the other networks that are connected to a particular network may be isolated from it except for the specific messages that are destined for hosts on the local network. Routers can recognize and manage protocols and multiple connections to networks. They need to be configured with addresses, protocols, and routes to particular hosts. Routers can usually only handle routing between networks that use the same protocol. They can route between networks that use different data-link layers such as Ethernet, Token Ring, and so forth, as long as they all use the same protocol.

SUMMARY

This chapter has examined the OSI model of networks which proposes that there are seven different layers with different functions to adequately describe the mechanisms of moving data from one network to another. Each of these seven layers has its own distinct functions. Use of some or all of the layers may be necessary to move data from one host to another. Several cases where only some of the layers were used to move data from one host to another were illustrated.

For further study, the following papers are of interest: J. P. Gray and T. B. McNeill, *IBM Systems Journal*, Vol. 18(2), 263–297(1979); P. E. Green, *IEEE Transactions on Communications*, Vol. 28(4), 413–423(1980); J. F. Shoch, Y. K. Dalal, D. D. Redell, and R. C. Crane, *Computer*, 10–27(August 1982); W. Stallings, *Computing Reviews*, Vol. 16(1), 3–41(1984); and H. Zimmerman, *IEEE Transactions on Communications*, Vol. 28(4), 425–432(1980).

Protocols of TCP/IP

15

INTRODUCTION

In this chapter TCP/IP is examined to see what its structure is and how it functions in light of the OSI layered model of communication networks discussed in Chapter 14. Each of the various protocols of TCP/IP is discussed in relation to its place in a layered model of computer networking. How data moves through this layered scheme is illustrated with particular reference to the units of information that each layer processes. The services the two protocols in the transport layer provide are compared and the way they are used by telnet is illustrated.

PHYSICAL MODEL OF A NETWORK

For two computers to communicate with each other there must be a physical pathway between them that messages can traverse. Two different models for this physical connection are possible: The first is that the two hosts reside in the same local network and the second is that the two hosts reside in different networks that are connected by gateways. Figure 15.1 shows schematically these two physical models.

a. First Model of Two Communicating Hosts

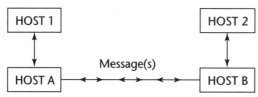

b. Second Model of Two Communicating Hosts

FIGURE 15.1 Two physical models of two communicating hosts.

In the first model messages can be sent directly from one host to another without any assistance from intermediaries, but in the second model the help of at least one extra host will be necessary for a message to get from Host 1 to Host 2. TCP/IP handles both types of communications.

For the first model, the connection between the two hosts is direct. The second model illustrates a type of connection usually called *virtual* in the sense that Host 1 and Host 2 believe that they are communicating directly with each other while in reality there is at least one and possibly several other hosts that are relaying the message. Virtual connections are shown with dashed lines to differentiate them from real connections. TCP/IP even provides for different routes through the network for successive messages. The next section will illustrate how TCP/IP can accomplish both kinds of connections.

LAYERS OF TCP/IP

If we examine TCP/IP as a layered data communications networking product, a simplified model, such as Figure 15.2, would show the various layers of TCP/IP. In this figure the name of the layer in the ISO model is shown on the left side and the main protocol that TCP/IP provides is shown on the right. This model of TCP/IP shows just five layers to the TCP/IP networking soft-

Application Layer	APPLICATIONS
Transport Layer	TRANSMISSION CONTROL PROTOCOL
Network Layer	INTERNET PROTOCOL
Data Link Layer	(NETWORK INTERFACE PROTOCOLS)
Physical Layer	(PHYSICAL NETWORKS)

Note: OSI Layers shown on the left side and the protocols TCP/IP provides for each layer on the right.

FIGURE 15.2 Model of TCP/IP layers compared with OSI model.

ware and not seven as the ISO standard would require. TCP/IP does not follow the ISO standard because neither a presentation layer nor a session layer is individually defined. TCP/IP applications provide the services of these two layers as necessary.

For the bottom two layers of the OSI model, data-link layer and physical layer, TCP/IP does not provide any specific protocol, but instead interfaces with whatever protocols are available.

TCP/IP is really a family of protocols, each of which is designed to solve a particular network communications problem. The view of TCP/IP layering in Figure 15.2 provides a simplified model while Figure 15.3 gives a more detailed view, again providing reference to the layers that the OSI model contains. The more detailed model illustrates that: For the network layer, there are a number of protocols provided by TCP/IP; for the transport layer there are two protocols provided by TCP/IP; and for the application layer, there are again a number of applications provided by TCP/IP. For the data-link layer and the physical layer, TCP/IP provides no new protocols, but instead interacts with the protocols that others provide.

To pass data from one computer to another, the data will move successively through the layers of the communications software system, as shown in Figure 15.4. Each layer performs specific functions that enable a message to move from one host through a network to another host and adds specific information to the message, as shown in Figure 15.5. If there are intervening hosts that must route the data through the network to another host, only the data-link layer and possibly the network layer of TCP/IP in the intervening hosts are involved, as shown in Figure 15.4(b).

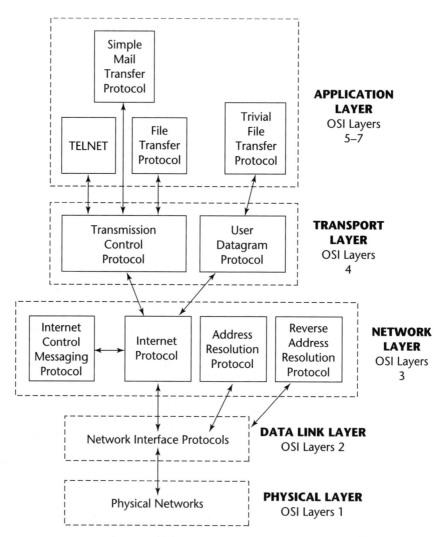

FIGURE 15.3 Protocols of TCP/IP.

Each layer on the sending host adds information to the message and each layer on the receiving host removes information from the message. This process is called *encapsulation*. Thus, the application layer will generate the data and pass that data to the transport layer. Then the transport layer on the sending host will add information to the front of the data and will pass that to the network layer. As each successive layer adds infor-

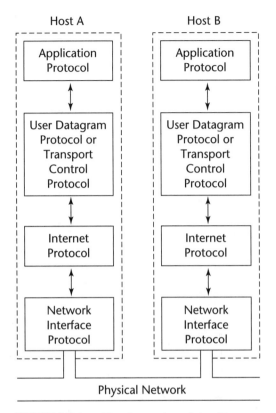

FIGURE 15.4a. Two layered models of two communicating hosts. First layered model of two hosts communicating with each other.

mation, the message will become longer. In the receiving host the information that was added by each layer in the sending host will be used and removed by the corresponding layer before passing the information to the next higher layer. A schematic diagram of how this would work is shown in Figure 15.5.

Routing data from one application on one node to another application on another node is done via a two-layered approach. At the transport layer, the address is a port number (16 bits long), which is the particular identification of an application on a particular node. It is unique to the application on the node and no other application can have that port number. This is a logical connecting point for an application.

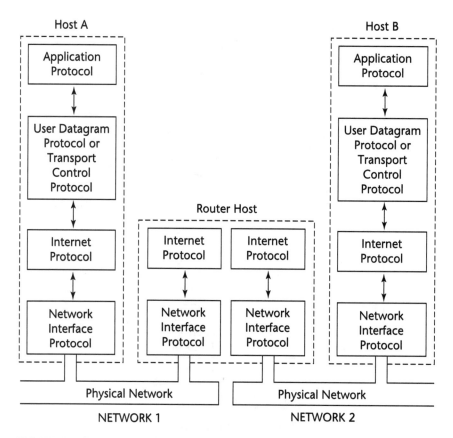

FIGURE 15.4b. Two layered models of two communicating hosts. Second layered model of two communicating hosts.

The actual node that the information is going to is specified in the next layer down, the network layer, which uses addresses that are 32 bits long and are usually called internet addresses. Each host is assigned at least one unique internet address. In the next layer down, the data-link layer, the address of the receiving host is translated to a physical address and passed onto the network to be communicated to the receiving host.

In the next sections, starting with the bottom layer and moving up the layers, we will examine the information each of these layered software protocols adds and how that information is used.

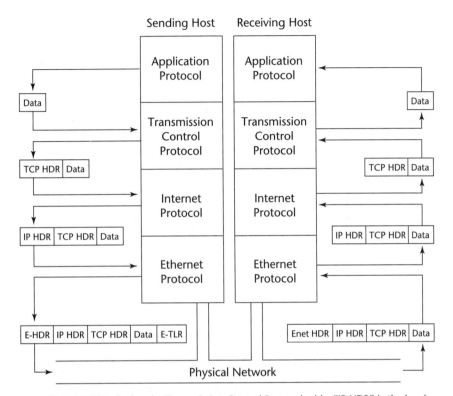

Note: "TCP HDR" is the header Transmission Control Protocol adds, "IP HDR" is the header Internet Protocol adds, "E-HDR" is the header, and "E-TLR" is the trailer that the Ethernet software adds.

FIGURE 15.5 Transmitting a message from one host to another.

DATA-LINK LAYER OF TCP/IP

The data-link layer of TCP/IP can use any variety of networking systems, such as Ethernet, Token Ring, and even X.25. This layer of the protocol attaches the appropriate header depending on what type of hardware/software is being used. Figure 15.5 illustrated how the Ethernet header (and trailer) would be added by the network layer if an Ethernet-based data-link layer were being used. Similar headers would be added by other data-link protocol methods. TCP/IP does not uniquely define this layer; instead, it uses any data-link layer that provides a communications pathway from the sending host to the receiving host.

NETWORK LAYER OF TCP/IP

For the network layer, OSI Layer 3, TCP/IP offers a variety of protocols, of which only the internet protocol (IP) offers the ability to move data between hosts. The other protocols offer special services to aid IP in its functions.

The internet protocol requires that each host in a network have a unique address, called the *internet address*. These internet addresses are registered in the /etc/hosts file or provided by a name service. Once the internet address of a host is known, it can be sent messages using the internet protocol. The IP attaches its header as the message is passed to the lower-level protocol as shown in Figure 15.5.

The internet protocol layer provides several other protocols that assist the internet protocol itself in its task of moving messages. Address Resolution Protocol (ARP) provides a method for translating internet addresses into hardware addresses and Reverse Address Resolution Protocol (RARP) provides a method for translating hardware addresses into internet addresses. Thus, messages bound to or coming from a host whose hardware address is known or whose internet address is known can be presented to the internet protocol for processing or to the datalink layer for sending to the destination host. Another protocol in this layer, Internet Control Message Protocol (ICMP), provides error-reporting services so that problems in delivering messages can be made known.

TRANSPORT LAYER OF TCP/IP

The transport layer provides services so that one application program on a particular host can communicate with another application program on a remote host. TCP/IP provides two protocols in the transport layer: One is a nonguaranteed datagram-based service which is called the User Datagram Protocol (UDP) and the other is a reliable data stream which is called Transmission Control Protocol (TCP). These two protocols offer different services as listed in Figure 15.6. A user application can

Service	UDP	TCP
Connection-oriented?	N	Y
Message Boundaries?	Y	N
Data Checksum?	Optional	Y
Positive Acknowledgment?	N	Y
Timeout and Retransmit?	N	Y
Duplicate Detection?	N	Y
Sequencing?	N	Y
Flow Control?	N	Y

FIGURE 15.6   UDP and TCP services compared.

choose which of these two protocols to use depending on which set of services that application needs.

The transport layer adds the address of the service on the remote host to the data the application layer generates. This address is called the port number and can be determined for well-known services such as mail, file transfer, and so forth, by examining a file called /etc/services. This port number is specific to the type of protocol (either UDP or TCP) that is being used and must be unique to the application.

For specific services provided by TCP/IP-based clients, you will have to determine their well-known port address by examining the /etc/services file or by using one of the system services to request the port number for a particular service. For example, the **ftp** server uses port number 21. To send a request to the **ftp** server, you would address your request to port number 21 on the host of interest.

As shown in Figure 15.3, there are two protocols that can be used for the transport layer (ISO Layer 4): TCP and UDP. Thus, there are two different methods for two user processes to pass data between each other. As an example of the use of one particular method, the TELNET application uses TCP as the transport layer protocol, as shown in Figure 15.7. Other applications use UDP. Which of the two protocols is used in the transport layer depends on which set of services the application needs.

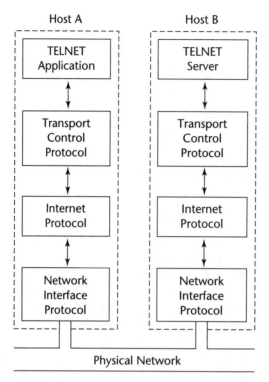

FIGURE 15.7 How TELNET uses TCP/IP protocols.

APPLICATION LAYER OF TCP/IP

The application layer of TCP/IP will appropriately format the data that is to be communicated to the receiving application layer and perform the services that are necessary. This data is then passed to the transport layer for further processing. The services provided by this layer include: (1) name services, so that pathways between hosts can be determined; (2) file transfer services, so that files can be transferred between dissimilar processors; (3) mail services, so that letters can be exchanged between users; and (4) telnet services, so that terminal devices on one host can interface with remote hosts. In addition, some TCP/IP implementations include remote command execution services so that commands can be executed on a host to which you are not connected.

UNITS OF INFORMATION IN EACH LAYER

The units of information that are handled by each of the layers in a TCP/IP network are indicated in Figure 15.8. The application layer creates data that it passes to the transport layer that the transport layer turns into messages which it passes to the network layer. The network layer will divide the messages into standard-sized pieces called *packets*. Finally the packets are broken into frames by the data-link layer and matched in size to the particular medium being used. Because TCP/IP networks pass packets between nodes of a network, these networks are often called **Packet Switched Networks**.

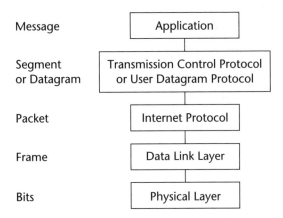

FIGURE 15.8 Units of information used by TCP/IP protocol layers.

Lower Level Header	Internet Protocol Hdr	Transport Header	Application Data

← – – – – – – – Frame – →

　　　　　← – – – – – – – – – Packet – – – – – – – – – – – →

　　　　　　　　　　　← – – – Datagram (UDP) ·– →
　　　　　　　　　　　　　　　　or
　　　　　　　　　　　← – – – Segment (TCP) – – →

FIGURE 15.9 Units of information during transmission of messages.

A slightly different way to examine this is illustrated in Figure 15.9, which shows how the message with all its headers will be partitioned by the various layers when they transmit it.

SUMMARY

This chapter examined how the layering that TCP/IP uses is applied to the task of moving information from one host to another. References to the OSI model provide a framework for the protocols that TCP/IP provides. Each of the layers that TCP/IP has together with the variety of protocols that TCP/IP provides are discussed in outline form. Chapters 5, 6, and 7 discuss in detail how each of protocols in TCP/IP operate. The units of information that each layer operates on are discussed.

One quite useful source of information is a book published by IBM: *Communication Concepts and Procedures for AIX Version 3 for RISC System/6000*, First edition, March 1990, Document Number SC23-2203 which describes in general terms how TCP/IP is viewed by IBM and what facilities are part of their TCP/IP implementation.

Internet Protocol: Network Layer Protocols

16

INTRODUCTION

The network layer of TCP/IP provides the services necessary to move data from one node to another node, even if the nodes are on different physical networks. To accomplish this goal, the layer contains one major protocol to move the data from node to node, the internet protocol (IP), and several other protocols (which will be discussed in Chapter 17) to solve other node-to-node communications problems.

In order to move data from one node to another efficiently, there are two services that this protocol layer must offer. First, a function must exist that can determine a route through the network to deliver the data to the uniquely identified remote host and secondly, functionality must be provided so that messages can be broken up into pieces if an intervening network is unable to handle the large size of the message. Both of these functions will be discussed, as well as the sending of messages to a group of hosts via two different methods.

OVERVIEW OF INTERNET PROTOCOL

Returning once again to a model of the TCP/IP protocols mapped against the functions required by the OSI model of net-

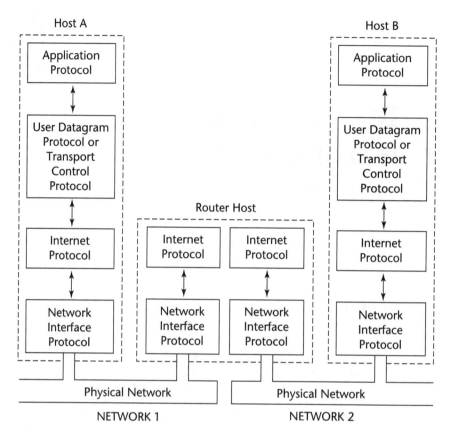

FIGURE 16.1 Layered model of two communicating hosts.

works we would see that the Network layer is the one which enables data to move from one node to another. As Figure 16.1 illustrates, the network layers on cooperating nodes are in communication with each other. Intermediate nodes in this model only need to have the network layer in order to perform their function of moving the data to another node which is logically closer to the destination. Higher and lower layers are only involved as requesters and servers.

The two major services that the internet protocol layer provides are addressing (to deliver messages from one host to another host) and fragmentation (to move messages through networks that have small packet sizes).

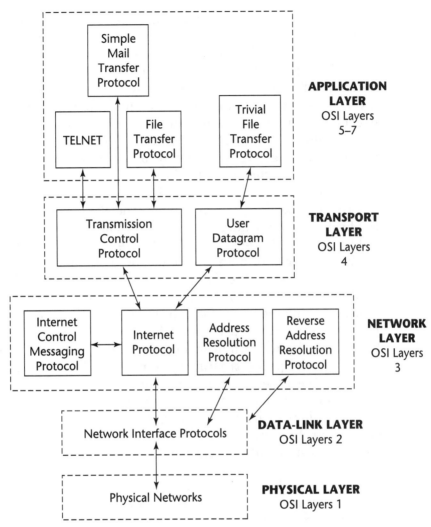

FIGURE 16.2   Internet protocols interaction with other TCP/IP protocols.

Figure 16.2 illustrates where the internet protocol fits in to a layered model of TCP/IP.

INTERNET PROTOCOL EXPLAINED

The internet protocol provides an unreliable connectionless method of delivering data from one host to another. It is unreliable because it does not guarantee delivery and provides no sequencing to even assure that the data packets are received in order. No acknowledgment is required of any participating hosts. It is connectionless because no initialization sequence is necessary for one host to connect with another using the IP layer. The data is packaged in a unit called a packet. Each packet of data is independent of every other packet of data.

As illustrated in Figure 16.2, the internet layer adds a header to the data that is passed to it from the transport layer before it passes that data to the data-link layer. The layout of this header is shown in Figure 16.3.

In the internet protocol header, the Version field identifies the format of the header used (usually the value 4). The Length field specifies the length of the header only in 32-bit words, while the length of both the header and the data measured in octets is carried in the Total Length field. The Type of Service field indicates the quality of service desired during the transmission of this message through the internet system. For example, a message can be designated for high or low delay, normal or high throughput, normal or high reliability. Priority messages can be given special treatment by network facilities if so indicated via the Type of Service field. Applications request a particular level of service when they pass their message to this layer.

The Identification field uniquely identifies this packet so that it can be distinguished from other packets; it is usually assigned when data is passed to the network layer from a

0	4	8	16	19	31
Version	Lngth	Type of Srvc	Total Length		
Identification			Flags	Fragment Offset	
Time to Live		Protocol	Header Checksum		
Source Address					
Destination Address					
Options					
Data					

FIGURE 16.3 Structure of the Internet protocol header.

higher layer. The Flags field indicates whether this message is fragmented and whether this is the last message fragment. The Fragment Offset field is the offset from the start of the original packet that this fragment is; it is used to rebuild the full message once all the fragments have been collected. This value is expressed in units of eight octets or 64 bits. The Protocol field specifies the next level protocol used in the data portion of this internet datagram. Some values for this field are shown in Figure 16.4.

The Time to Live field specifies how long the datagram will be stored on the network before it is destroyed. A time limit must be specified so that if there is an error on the network and some fragment is lost, the other pieces of the original message will be destroyed at some later time and not continue to use the resources of the network. In addition, datagrams can be created for destinations that can cause the datagram to endlessly loop through the internet using the resources of the internet. The current recommended default time is 64.

The Header Checksum field is used to provide error checking on the header by itself. The Source Address and Destination Address are the Internet addresses of the hosts of interest. The Options field is used for specifying routing options, security

Decimal	Protocol
0	Reserved
1	Internet Control Message
2	Internet Group Management
3	Gateway-to-Gateway
4	IP in IP (encapsulation)
5	Stream
6	Transmission Control
7	UCL
8	Exterior Gateway Protocol
9	any private interior gateway

FIGURE 16.4 Some assigned Internet protocol numbers.

options, and network testing. One setting of the options field requests that the route that this packet takes be recorded in the packet. Another option indicates that the routing through the network is specified in this packet and should be used.

FRAGMENTATION OF PACKETS

Individual routers may have to change the size of the message because it may not be possible for a particular router to handle the largest size message. The identification, offset, length, and

Original Datagram:
   Data Length = 850
   Identification = 1
   Offset = 0
   More = 0

First Fragment:
   Data Length = 240
   Identification = 1
   Offset = 0
   More = 1

Second Fragment:
   Data Length = 240
   Identification = 1
   Offset = 30
   More = 1

Third Fragment:
   Data Length = 240
   Identification = 1
   Offset = 60
   More = 1

Last Fragment:
   Data Length = 130
   Identification = 1
   Offset = 90
   More = 0

FIGURE 16.5 Fragmentation of packet into smaller messages.

flags fields are used together to enable segmentation of packets as they travel through the network from source to destination. The identification is assigned when the packet is initially passed to the network layer to be transmitted to the destination host. At a particular intermediate router, it may be necessary to break up the packet into smaller fragments. This process is called *fragmentation*. The original message is divided into shorter size pieces, transmitting each as a different datagram. Each datagram is created with the same header as the first message, but it would have an offset that points at where this part of the message would be placed when reconstructing the original packet. If this was the last piece of the original packet, the *more* flag would be off. The offset flag is counted in units of eight octets (or 64 bits). As an example, Figure 16.5 shows breaking up a larger datagram into a number of smaller ones.

The identification field is used by the receiving host to gather together all the various pieces of the message to be reassembled. The offset is used to place the pieces in the correct order to reconstruct the original message.

ROUTING MESSAGES FROM ONE NODE TO ANOTHER

Routing is accomplished by maintaining routing tables in each station that indicate for each destination network the next router this packet should be sent to. The routing is dynamic and the router needs to be able to "learn" the shortest pathway to a particular network. The internet protocol provides several ways for the router to "learn" about its surrounding networks.

One of the option fields found in the internet protocol header requests that each router record in the packet what routers were traversed in moving this packet from source to destination. This kind of information could be used by intermediate routers to understand what pathways through the network are used to reach certain hosts.

INTERNET ADDRESSING

Each host in a network must have a unique address assigned to it in order for messages to be uniquely sent to a particular host.

These addresses (called *internet addresses*) are 32 bits long and are usually displayed in the format X.X.X.X where X is eight bits long and can have any value from 0 to 255. Addresses in this format are often called *dotted decimal* addresses. Each host also has a unique name assigned to it; that name and the host's internet address can be used interchangeably in sending messages to a particular host if the name and address have been registered in the /etc/hosts file or a name server is available. For more information, see Chapter 12.

Internet addresses are divided into several classes, each of which is illustrated in Figure 16.6. The first five bits in the address are used to indicate which class of address is meant. Class A addresses have "0" as the value of the first bit, Class B

```
0  1  2  3  4         8              16                24              31
┌─┬──────────────┬─────────────────────────────────────────────────────┐
│0│ Network ID (7 bits) │          Host ID (24 bits)                    │
└─┴──────────────┴─────────────────────────────────────────────────────┘
```
a. Class A Address

```
0  1  2  3  4         8              16                24              31
┌──┬──────────────────────────┬──────────────────────────────────────┐
│1  0│  Network ID (14 bits)   │         Host ID (16 bits)            │
└──┴──────────────────────────┴──────────────────────────────────────┘
```
b. Class B Address

```
0  1  2  3  4         8              16                24              31
┌─────┬──────────────────────────────────────────┬──────────────────┐
│1  1  0│         Network ID (21 bits)            │  Host ID (8 bits) │
└─────┴──────────────────────────────────────────┴──────────────────┘
```
c. Class C Address

```
0  1  2  3  4         8              16                24              31
┌──────┬─────────────────────────────────────────────────────────────┐
│1  1  1  0│          Multicast Address (28 bits)                     │
└──────┴─────────────────────────────────────────────────────────────┘
```
d. Class D Address

```
0  1  2  3  4         8              16                24              31
┌────────┬───────────────────────────────────────────────────────────┐
│1  1  1  1  0│       Reserved for Future Use (27 bits)               │
└────────┴───────────────────────────────────────────────────────────┘
```
e. Class E Address

FIGURE 16.6 Various classes of Internet addresses.

addresses have "1 0" as the value of the first two bits, Class C addresses have "1 1 0" as the value of the first three bits in the address, Class D addresses have "1 1 1 0" as the value of the first four bits in the address, and Class E addresses have "1 1 1 1 0" as the value of the first five bits in the address. Thus, addresses that start with a value between 1 and 126 are Class A addresses (addresses that start with 0 or 127 are special addresses and are discussed later). Class B addresses have starting values between 128 and 191, while Class C addresses have starting values between 192 and 223. Class D addresses cover the range from 224 to 239, while Class E addresses cover the range from 240 to 255.

Using dotted decimal addressing for example, "1.2.255.4" is a Class A address, "129.30.3.30" is a Class B address, and "193.33.33.33" is a Class C address. Class A addresses are for networks that have lots of hosts on a single network while Class C addresses would be for a network with fewer hosts.

Only 126 different Class A networks can exist with each network having more than 16 million (256*256*256) hosts on it. The values of 0 and 127 are reserved for special purposes. With such a limited number of these kinds of networks available, only very large networks use this type of addressing. Since most networks do not have that many hosts, this type of addressing is for networks that are organized by subnets (see later discussion).

Up to 16,384 (64*256) different Class B networks can be created with 65,536 (256*256) hosts on each network. While more than 65,000 may seem to be a large number of hosts for a particular network, some company-wide networks will have easily this many hosts where many terminals (really diskless workstations) will be networked alongside the servers. Subnets will be useful for this kind of network, too.

More than 2 million (32*256*256) different Class C networks can be created with only 256 hosts on each network. For a small company or other institution this type of addressing would be appropriate. Subnets can be used here, too, to simplify routing tables.

Class D addresses do not identify networks but instead are used to identify special addressing modes. The principal use is for multicasting (see later discussion). Class E addresses are reserved for future use and have been used for some experimental addresses.

Internet addresses are assigned by a central agency so that an international network (of smaller networks) can be created with each network having a unique address. (See Appendix A for more information on the agency that manages this process.)

When setting up a network that does not intend to communicate with networks in the "outside world," an institution can choose any class of network addressing to use. When communicating with a network in the "outside world," an institution will have to abide by the addressing standards imposed by that network's administrative group. For the national networks such as Uunet, Bitnet, and so forth, a central agency (the SRI corporation) assigns network addresses to ensure that the addressing will be unique.

Hosts may have more than one address if they are connected to more than one network. These kinds of multiaddressed hosts, sometimes called multihomed hosts, are usually gateways or bridges to other networks. They will usually contain more than one network interface board and may support more than one protocol or more than one network medium. In this way, for example, Token Ring networks can be connected to Ethernet networks.

Since an internet address consists of a network id and a host id, gateways only need to know the location of other networks, not the location of every other host on that network in order to correctly route a message to another network.

SUBNET ADDRESSING

An organization with an assigned internet address can subdivide the available host address space in any way that it chooses. One possible way is to create *subnets* or networks within networks. The goal of any network approach is to be able to add hosts with a minimum of disruption to the rest of the network. Forming subnets provides the ability to add hosts easily to a network that contains a number of gateways.

0 1 2 3 4	8	16	24	31
1 0	Network ID (14 bits)	Subnet ID (8 bits)	Host ID (8 bits)	

FIGURE 16.7   Class B Internet address with an 8-bit subnet id.

In a networking system gateways need to have knowledge of where every host is located so that when a message needs to be sent to a particular host, the gateway will know a pathway to that host. Adding a new host requires that *every* routing table in each gateway must be updated. If you are setting up an addressing scheme for Class B internet addresses using subnets, for example, one could use eight bits of the host id as the subnet id as shown in Figure 16.7. The gateway can figure out what route to use to send a message to any particular host without having knowledge of each individual host by just examining the subnet id. In this example, a Class B type of internet address is used. Using a subnet address of eight bits allows for 254 subnets (the values of 0 and 255 are reserved), each of which can have up to 254 different hosts on it (usually values of 0 and 255 are not used for host addressing).

One way to illustrate the principle of using subnet addresses is to examine Figure 16.8 which shows a network with several hosts. Notice that Host 4 and Host 7 are gateways connecting two separate networks.

How would addresses be assigned to the hosts in this network? A simple way would be to assign the addresses in numerical order as shown in Figure 16.9.

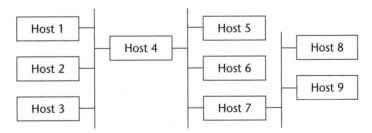

FIGURE 16.8   Typical network with nine hosts.

Name of Host	Internet Address
Host 1	131.3.3.1
Host 2	131.3.3.2
Host 3	131.3.3.3
Host 4	131.3.3.4
	131.3.3.5
Host 5	131.3.3.6
Host 6	131.3.3.7
Host 7	131.3.3.8
	131.3.3.9
Host 8	131.3.3.10
Host 9	131.3.3.11

FIGURE 16.9 First table of hosts and addresses.

If we were to create subnets, we could create addresses that would allow the gateways to know where to send a message without examining the entire network table. Figure 16.10 illustrates what the network addresses would be if a number of subnets were created.

If Host 1 sends a message to Host 8, the gateways only need to examine the subnet part of the address to determine how routing through the network would go. Addition of another host in subnet 3, for example, would not require changing the routing tables at all.

Every host in a network has to be able to determine the length of the subnet id field. One type of internet protocol (ICMP) has two special message types for this purpose. It is convenient for subnets to use contiguous bits for the subnet number of a network, but this is not a requirement. ICMP address mask request and reply messages enable a network to use noncontiguous bits for a subnet mask and to be able to inform other networks of their use. See Chapter 17 for more details on how ICMP messages work.

Name of Host	Subnet ID	Host ID	Internet Address
Host 1	1	1	131.3.1.1
Host 2	1	2	131.3.1.2
Host 3	1	3	131.3.1.3
Host 4	1	4	131.3.1.4
	2	1	131.3.2.1
Host 5	2	2	131.3.2.2
Host 6	2	3	131.3.2.3
Host 7	2	4	131.3.2.4
	3	1	131.3.3.1
Host 8	3	2	131.3.3.2
Host 9	3	3	131.3.3.3

FIGURE 16.10   Second table of host addresses using subnet addressing.

BROADCASTING MESSAGES

Hosts sometimes need to find information about a network or about a host without knowing exactly which host has that information. For example, a diskless workstation may not know its own internet address and may want to request some other host to notify it of its proper internet address. In addition, one host might have information that an entire group of hosts should have. For example, one host might have determined that a particular host is now operating as a gateway to another network and any message addressed to that network should be sent to this particular host. How can one host inform others of its network knowledge? One method would be to send a message to each and every host with the information of interest. Or, if information was needed, the request for information could be in a message that was sent in turn to each host until the information was received. This approach would lead to a flood of messages sent to a range of different hosts in order to gain some information about the network; this would not be an efficient way to send information around a network. Instead, a separate class of addressing rules was created with the purpose that any host that fits the addressing criteria can reply to the request for information or receive the information in the message. This messaging methodology is called *broadcasting*.

The following set of addressing rules defines which hosts are being addressed when broadcasting messages (these addresses can only be used as destination addresses):

- 255.255.255.255 denotes a broadcast message to *all* hosts on a *local* hardware network; these messages must not be forwarded to any other network through a gateway.
- 36.255.255.255 denotes a broadcast to *all* hosts on the *specific network* #36. If the message is a request for information, any host on network #36 can reply. If this network is using subnet addressing, this message is a broadcast to all subnets on network #36.
- 36.40.255.255 denotes a broadcast to *all* hosts on the *specific subnet* #40 on the *specific network* #36. (Address 36.40.255.255 is a Class A network and, thus, "40" cannot be part of the network address. As a further example, the address 195.40.255.255 is a broadcast to all hosts on the network 195.40 because this is a Class C address.)
- 127.0.0.1 denotes a broadcast to the *local host* only and acts as a local loopback address. Any messages sent to this address must not be sent out on the network, but instead are echoed back to the host.

The following set of rules defines special addresses that can be used as source addresses in a broadcast message:

- 0.0.0.0 denotes *this* host on *this* network. This special is used by a workstation that does not know its Internet address in a message that requests information about its own Internet address. (See the ICMP discussion in Chapter 17.)
- 0.0.0.27 denotes a *specified* host on *this* network. This special address can be used by hosts that do not know the network number (or subnet number) that they are part of.

For networks that are using subnet addressing, a broadcast to all hosts on a subnet would be to put in all 1s as the host address. If the subnet addressing is such as in the network in Figure 16.10 given earlier, then a broadcast to subnet #3 would use a destination address of 131.3.3.255.

MULTICASTING MESSAGES

A multicast message is one that is transmitted to a group of hosts on a network. The constitution of a group of hosts is dynamic; hosts may join and leave a group at any time. Multicast messages can even be sent to groups of hosts that are not on the local network. Host group addresses are those with "1110" as the high-order four bits (what was called Class D addresses earlier). In dotted decimal notation these group addresses range from 224.0.0.0 to 239.255.255.255. Two addresses in this range are special: 224.0.0.0 is guaranteed not to be assigned to any group and 224.0.0.1 is assigned to the permanent group of all IP hosts that will both receive and send multicast messages (usually gateways). Some of the currently assigned group addresses are listed in Figure 16.11. Other permanent groups will be assigned by the Internet Architecture Board as needed. To send a multicast message, simply code in the address of one of the destination groups as the destination address and otherwise treat the message in a standard way.

To handle group-oriented messages, the Internet Group Management Protocol (IGMP) was developed. This protocol is considered part of the IP layer of TCP/IP protocol suite. Two of the new operations added permit hosts to join a host group or to delete themselves from a host group. In addition, a Host Membership Query message may be used to determine if a particular host is a member of a particular group and a Host Membership Report message will be sent when the membership of a group changes.

INTERNET PROTOCOL NEXT GENERATION (IPNG)

Earlier in the chapter, the rules for creating an IP address were discussed. The length of an IP address is fixed at 32 bits and this limits the maximum number of addresses that are possible.

Multicast Address	Assigned to:
224.0.0.0	Reserved
224.0.0.1	All systems on this subnet
224.0.0.2	All routers on this subnet
224.0.0.3	Unassigned
224.0.0.4	DVMRP routers
224.0.0.5	OSPFIGP all routers
224.0.0.6	OSPFIGP designated routers
224.0.0.7	ST routers
224.0.0.8	ST hosts
224.0.0.9	RIP2 routers
224.0.0.10-224.0.0.255	Unassigned
224.0.1.0	VMTP managers group
224.0.1.1	NTP (Network Time Protocol)
224.0.1.2	SGI-Dogfight]
224.0.1.3	Rwhod
224.0.1.6	NSS—Name Service Server
224.0.1.9	MTP Multicast Transport Protocol
224.0.1.10-224.0.1.255	Unassigned
224.0.2.1	"rwho" group (BSD) (unofficial)
224.1.0.0-224.1.255.255	ST multicast groups
224.2.0.0-224.2.255.255	Multimedia conference calls

FIGURE 16.11 Assigned Internet multicast group addresses.

Even worse, the method of creating classes of addresses limits further the maximum number of networks that will have different addresses by removing the large blocks of addresses from being assigned.

The explosive growth of the Internet has been well documented and has led to several problems which can be traced to the IP addressing scheme. These problems are: not enough unassigned addresses (the overseers of the Internet expect to run out of addresses in the next ten years) and the rapidly growing size of the routing tables in routing networks. The first problem is caused by the limitation on the size of the IP address while the second problem is due to the fact that IP addressing is not hierarchical and a routing node has to maintain extensive information so as to know where in the Internet another node is located. In addition, the current IP definition has no defined method of securing the information in a message. Commercial use of the Internet requires some method of securing information in a message and currently all the security methods are grafted onto the current IP scheme.

To solve these problems, the developers of the Internet have proposed a new IP layer standard called Internet Protocol next generation or more familiarly, *IPng*. The first change in this standard from the current IP standard would be to increase the length of an IP address to 128 bits. This lengthening of the IP address will enable addresses to be assigned hierarchically which will address the problem of the size of the routing tables in a router. A second change is the addition of encryption and authentication methods that will be usable in the internetwork layer. Some details concerning management of the encryption keys have not been fully described but the addition of security features to this layer is specified. This new standard for the internetwork layer will be developed over the next few years with the expectation that support for some of these features would be available within five years.

SUMMARY

In this chapter the functionality of the internet protocol has been examined with emphasis on the message fragmentation and addressing functions that the internet protocol performs. An example of message fragmentation was used to illustrate how messages are fragmented when moving through networks that have smaller message sizes. The layout of the internet header was discussed with emphasis on the way particular fields in the header are used. The various classes of Internet addresses are illustrated and subnet addressing is shown to simplify routing tables. Addresses used for broadcasting and multicasting messages were examined to determine how to create an address that addresses only those hosts of interest.

The complete discussion of the internet protocol is found in RFC 791. Several additional RFCs cover various addressing issues including subnets (RFC 917), broadcasting (RFC 922), and multicasting (RFC 1112). For lists of the assigned values for the protocol field, the version field, the multicast addresses, and the type-of-service values, RFC 1240 "Assigned Numbers" should be examined.

Other Internet Protocols: ARP, RARP, and ICMP

INTRODUCTION

As discussed in Chapter 16, the internet protocol is used to move data from node to node. Problems that can interfere with this data movement are managed by a group of associated protocols that interact with the internet protocol as shown in Figure 17.1.

Address Resolution Protocol (ARP) offers the network interface protocols in the data-link layer the capability of translating software addresses to hardware addresses; Reverse Address Resolution Protocol (RARP) provides the ability to translate hardware addresses into software addresses. Internet Control Message Protocol (ICMP) provides many of the error-reporting mechanisms that can be used to regulate the performance of the network.

ADDRESS RESOLUTION PROTOCOL (ARP)

The internet address of a node is a software-assigned set of numbers, but the "real" address that the data-link layer software knows nodes by is a hardware address. For example, every

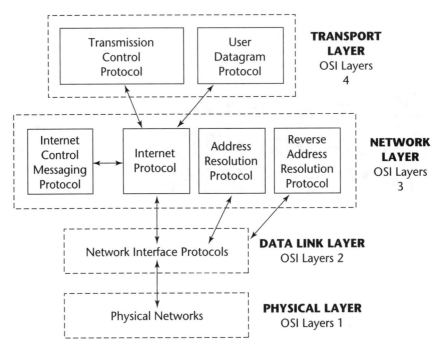

FIGURE 17.1 Internet protocol interaction with other TCP/IP protocols.

Ethernet transceiver has an address which is unique and that address will need to be used by the data-link layer of other nodes to send messages to that node. For other hardware-based networks, different addressing schemes exist to solve the same problem: addressing messages to the desired host using its hardware address. The network layer of TCP/IP uses the internet address as its method to address a particular node. But how does the data-link layer translate an internet address into a hardware address, such as the Ethernet address?

Giving each node an internet address that is used by the Internet Protocol only, enables the Internet protocol layer to be isolated from the hardware and data-link layers that use their own methods of addressing nodes in a network. Thus, the internet protocol is not dependent on any particular hardware addressing scheme. Unfortunately, this independence is not without its cost: Some service must be available that will provide the hardware address of a node in a network if its internet address is known. To solve this problem for the internet protocol, the Address Resolution Protocol (ARP) protocol was developed.

ARP is a protocol which maps internet addresses to hardware addresses. Even though the ARP function is provided as a required part of the IP layer, the data-link layer uses the ARP function directly.

Nodes that will be communicated with are often registered in a file which contains their internet address but not their hardware address. See, for example, the discussion of the /etc/hosts file in Chapter 8. Yet the data-link layer will need the hardware address to send messages to the correct node. The ARP server can be requested by the data-link layer to inform it what the hardware address of the internet host is. The composition of the data packet that ARP uses to determine the translation is shown in Figure 17.2.

In order to provide the ability of ARP to support different hardware platforms (and thus, the isolate internet protocol from the hardware and data-link layers), the ARP data packet contains flags to indicate what kind of hardware and which protocol is being serviced and what length each of their addresses is. ARP can manage translation of any of the various hardware addresses because the length of the hardware address is specified in the request and reply packet itself. The HdwrLngth field indicates the length of each hardware address (shown in Figure 17.2 as N bytes long) and the SftwrLngth field indicates the

0	8	16	31
Type of Hardware		Type of Protocol	
HdwrLngth	SftwrLngth	Message Opcode	
Hardware address of sender (N Bytes)			
Protocol address of sender (M Bytes)			
Hardware Address of target (N Bytes)			
Protocol Address of Target (M Bytes)			

FIGURE 17.2 ARP data packet.

length of each protocol address (shown in Figure 17.2 as M bytes long). For example, Ethernet hardware addresses are 48 bits in length while other hardware addresses are somewhat shorter. Figure 17.3 lists some hardware types and protocols that are supported by ARP.

For ARP to operate as an address translator, only two function codes are needed: (1) ARP REQUEST code which asks for address translation, and (2) ARP REPLY code which indicates this packet contains the reply to an ARP request. Both the hardware and software addresses of the target host and the sender host are contained in the packet.

For ARP requests a packet will be sent out which contains the internet address of the sender (and the hardware address of the sender) and the internet address of the target with no hardware address filled in. The opcode is set to "ARP REQUEST." Such a packet using Ethernet as the hardware layer is illustrated in Figure 17.4.

This packet will be broadcast to the network. When such an address resolution packet is received by the target node, the receiving Ethernet module will forward that packet to the ARP process on that node to reply to. Other nodes may record the address of the sending node, but they will not reply to the message, even if they have the information requested. Thus, ARP operates in the same layer as the internet protocol, as an adjunct to it. The ARP process that receives this packet will move the sender addresses into the target addresses and will fill in the hardware and internet protocol addresses of the sender with its own hardware/protocol addresses as shown in Figure 17.5. The opcode of the ARP packet is changed to ARP REPLY and the message is sent back to the originating node.

In addition, the ARP process will add the hardware address, protocol address, and protocol type to a table that the ARP process maintains. If this set of information is already in the table, that entry is updated. This action will allow ARP to resolve the next address request, if it is necessary to do so in the future. For large complicated networks with many nodes, preloading this translation table might be more efficient than having ARP REQUEST and REPLY messages generated and floating around the network. A command can be used to inform

Hardware Type	Description
1	Ethernet (10Mb)
2	Experimental Ethernet (3Mb)
3	Amateur Radio AX.25
4	Proteon ProNET Token Ring
5	Chaos
6	IEEE 802 Networks
7	ARCNET
8	Hyperchannel
9	Lanstar
10	Autonet Short Address
11	LocalTalk
12	LocalNet (IBM PCNet or SYTEK LocalNET)
13	Ultra link
14	SMDS
15	Frame Relay
16	Asynchronous Transmission Mode (ATM)

Protocol Type		Description
Dec	Hex	
512	0200	XEROX PUP
513	0201	PUP Addr Trans
1536	0600	XEROX NS IDP
2048	0800	DOD IP
2049	0801	X.75 Internet
2050	0802	NBS Internet
2051	0803	ECMA Internet
2052	0804	Chaosnet
2053	0805	X.25 Level 3
2054	0806	ARP
2055	0807	XNS Compatability
2184	0888	Xyplex
2304	0900	Ungermann-Bass net debugr
2560	0A00	Xerox IEEE802.3 PUP
4096	1000	Berkeley Trailer nego
4097	1001	Berkeley Trailer encap/IP
5632	1600	Valid Systems
16962	4242	PCS Basic Block Protocol
21000	5208	BBN Simnet
24576	6000	DEC Unassigned (Exp.)
24579	6003	DEC DECNET Phase IV Route
(and many more)		

FIGURE 17.3   ARP-supported hardware and protocol types.

0	8	16	31
0	1	8	0
6	4	0	1
11	11	11	11
11	11	192	11
11	11	0	0
0	0	0	0
193	36	20	20

FIGURE 17.4 Sample ARP request packet for an Ethernet LAN.

ARP of known software address and hardware address couplets. This command takes the form

```
arp -s InternetAddr HardwareAddr
```

where "InternetAddr" is the internet address and "Hard-wareAddr" is the hardware address for that host. Using a set of these commands when starting up a network will eliminate ARP message traffic.

With the length of the hardware address and the length of the protocol address included in the ARP packets, support of different types of hardware addresses is possible. In addition, the

0	8	16	31
0	1	8	0
6	4	0	1
11	11	11	11
11	11	192	11
11	11	0	0
0	0	0	0
193	36	20	20

FIGURE 17.5 Sample ARP reply packet for an Ethernet LAN.

ARP module need not know what hardware method is used because it gets its hardware addresses from the messages it receives from other ARP modules.

Since ARP requests are broadcast to all nodes on a network, it is not an error if a particular node does not reply. All ARP requests received are used to maintain a translation table that contains protocol type, protocol address, hardware type, and hardware address for nodes in the network. If the target protocol address or hardware address matches the protocol address of a particular node, that node must reply to the ARP request packet. If the node whose internet address is in the message fails to reply, it is assumed that the node is no longer in service. The ARP translation table can be displayed by entering the command

```
arp -a
```

and the display will look like

```
host1.localcomp.com (198.129.31.3) at 2:60:8c:42:29:93
   [ethernet]
host2.localcomp.com (198.129.31.4) at 2:60:8c:2f:d3:2b
   [ethernet]
host3.localcomp.com (198.129.31.5) at 0:80:2d:0:2f:e9
   [ethernet]
host4.localcomp.com (198.129.31.6) at aa:0:4:0:1:4
   [ethernet]
host5.localcomp.com (198.129.31.7) at 2:60:8c:a4:69:30
   [ethernet]
```

indicating for a remote host what its internet address and hardware type and address are.

REVERSE ADDRESS RESOLUTION PROTOCOL (RARP)

How can a node in a network determine its own internet address if all it knows is its hardware address? To solve this problem, Reverse Address Resolution Protocol (RARP) was developed.

RARP is a protocol that will map hardware addresses to internet addresses. In particular, diskless workstations need to know the hardware address of the node that will be booting them up. In addition, the data-link layer will need to translate hardware addresses into internet addresses so that it can determine which host sent a particular message. This translation is provided by using the Reverse Address Resolution Protocol.

Some diskless workstations that are loaded by other workstations in a network may not know their own internet addresses. In order for the loading of their software to succeed (usually using tftp services), the internet address of the workstation needs to be determined. The RARP server can be requested to provide this address. The basic packet that RARP uses is the same one that ARP used as illustrated in Figure 17.4. One additional opcode (3) is used to inform the target of the message that RARP address translation is needed. A second additional opcode (4) is needed to inform the sender of the initial RARP message that this message contains the response to the RARP request.

A diskless workstation usually knows its own hardware address and the hardware address of the device that will load its software, usually called the *boot* device. But it won't know the internet address of its boot device and usually won't know its own internet address. RARP provides the ability for the diskless workstation to send out a packet with just the information that it knows and get back a reply that contains the missing information.

The node desiring to determine its own internet address would broadcast a packet that is like the one in Figure 17.6.

0	8	16	31
0	1	8	0
6	4	0	3
11	22	33	44
55	66	0	0
0	0	44	44
44	44	44	44
0	0	0	0

FIGURE 17.6 Sample RARP request reverse packet for an Ethernet LAN.

0	8	16	31
0	1	8	0
6	4	0	4
44	44	44	44
44	44	193	3
4	5	11	22
33	44	55	66
196	6	7	8

FIGURE 17.7   Sample RARP reply reverse packet for an Ethernet LAN.

In this example, a node which has a hardware address of 11.22.33.44.55.66 is requesting that the node whose hardware address is 44.44.44.44.44.44 provide its internet address. Ethernet addresses and internet addresses are used as examples. The reply packet as illustrated in Figure 17.7 indicates that its internet address is 196.6.7.8 and the internet address of the node that was requested for information is 193.3.4.5.

INTERNET CONTROL MESSAGE PROTOCOL (ICMP)

The Internet Control Message Protocol (ICMP) is handled by the TCP/IP protocol itself and not user processes. It is used by TCP/IP to report errors and transfer control information between gateways and hosts. ICMP uses IP as a higher level protocol, even though it is an integral part of IP. ICMP encapsulates IP packets just as the data layer will. Figure 17.8 details the contents of ICMP messages. The Type field indicates which kind of message this is and the various possible types are listed in Figure 17.9. The Code field denotes a particular kind of error for an error response and has other values for other message types. The Checksum field is used to ensure that the entire ICMP message has not been corrupted. For a number of messages, Identifier and Sequence Number fields are used to match request messages with reply messages.

0	8	16	31
Type	Code	Checksum	
Different uses for different message types			
Internet Protocol Header including Originating Address and Destination Address ~ ~			
64 Bits of Original Data Packet			

FIGURE 17.8 Internet Control Message Protocol (ICMP) packet.

Type	Message Use
0	Echo Reply
3	Destination Unreachable
4	Source Quench
5	Redirect
8	Echo
11	Time Exceeded
12	Parameter Problem
13	Timestamp
14	Timestamp Reply
15	Information Request
16	Information Reply
17	Address Mask Request
18	Address Mask Reply
A1	Address Format Request
A2	Address Format Reply

FIGURE 17.9 Internet Control Message Protocol packet types.

The different message types function as follows:

- **Destination Unreachable** message is sent by a gateway to the source address of an IP data packet if that message cannot be delivered to the intended node. A code in the message is set to indicate which component in the network is unreachable and whether the problem is due to unavailability of the node or an incorrect route to the node.

- **Time Exceeded** message is sent when a packet must be discarded because it could not be delivered in the time required.
- **Source Quench** message is sent by the host or gateway when it is receiving messages at too rapid a rate or if its buffers are becoming filled and it will be forced to discard messages. Nodes that receive these messages are supposed to cut back the rate at which they are sending data packets or the receiving node will be forced to discard packets.
- **Parameter Problem** message is sent by a gateway or host when it discovers a problem with one of the header parameters that will cause the message to be discarded and not delivered.
- **Redirect Message** is sent by a gateway when that gateway determines that the host that sent the message and another gateway that is on the same network as the source host is closer to the destination host than this gateway is.
- **Echo** message is sent by a gateway or a host to another gateway or host.
- **Echo Reply** message is returned by the destination host or gateway to indicate that gateway or host is still operating.
- **Timestamp** message is sent by a host to another host.
- **Timestamp Reply** message is returned by that host so that the time it takes for a message to get from one host to another can be determined.
- **Information and Information Reply** messages are sent by a host to determine its own network number.
- **Address Format Request** message is sent by a host or a gateway to learn the number of bits in the subnet part of the internet address for a particular network.
- **Address Format Reply** message contains the number of bits in the subnet part of the address in the code field in the ICMP message.
- **Address Mask Request** message is sent by a host or a gateway to determine what subnet mask is being used on a subnet on a network. The host or gateway that knows the subnet mask will send the subnet mask to the requesting host or gateway in an **Address Mask Reply** message. (It is not

enough to know the number of bits in the subnet mask because it is entirely possible that the subnet mask is not a contiguous set of bits.)

SUMMARY

This chapter has focused on the various protocols in the internet layer other than the internet protocol. Each of these protocols assists the internet protocol so that the internet protocol can move data from one node to another. Address Resolution Protocol translates internet addresses into hardware addresses that the network interface protocols can use. Reverse Address Resolution Protocol translates network interface protocols into internet addresses. In addition, reporting of errors in the network is provided by the Internet Control Message Protocol.

Address Resolution Protocol is described in RFC 826, Reverse Address Resolution Protocol is described in RFC 903, and Internet Control Message Protocol in RFC 792. The various Assigned Numbers for TCP/IP are listed in RFC 1340 and forms the basis for Figure 17.3. Some subnet addressing issues are discussed in RFC 917 and 950.

User Datagram and Transmission Control Protocols: Transport Layer Protocols

INTRODUCTION

In the layered view of TCP/IP, the User Datagram Protocol (UDP) and Transmission Control Protocol (TCP) provide the service that application programs need: raw data delivery. As shown in Figure 3.6, UDP and TCP provide different kinds of services. Applications can choose which protocol provides the kind of services that they need. Figure 18.1 illustrates which protocol is used for several applications and displays how UDP and TCP fit into this model of TCP/IP. Both UDP and TCP use the Internet protocol as the underlying protocol.

This chapter is concerned with examining UDP and TCP and their functionality and structure in order to understand how each of these protocols provides the various services that it does.

USER DATAGRAM PROTOCOL (UDP)

The User Datagram Protocol (UDP) provides a method for one application to send a message to another application on another

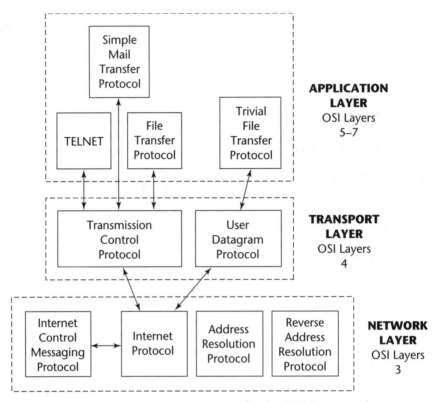

FIGURE 18.1   How UDP and TCP interact with other TCP/IP protocols.

network without requiring that the destination application be active when the message is sent to the destination network. UDP is a datagram-based protocol which does not guarantee delivery and does not guarantee protection against duplicate datagrams. The one advantage of UDP is that it requires a minimum of services to move data from one host to another. The structure of the UDP packet is shown in Figure 18.2.

In the UDP header the Source Port is used to provide identification of the source of the message. This field does not need to be filled in because there is no requirement that the host that receives this data reply to the source of the data. If this field is not valid, it must be filled with zero. The Destination Port field is used to provide identification of the destination port. The port for a particular application can be determined by examining a

0	16	31
Source Port	Destination Port	
Length	Checksum	

FIGURE 18.2   Structure of the User Datagram Protocol header.

table of well-known ports. The overall Length of the packet (in octets) includes the length of the UDP header as well as the length of the data portion of the datagram. The Checksum field checks the entire datagram including the header and the data.

This is a connectionless message delivery; UDP considers the message delivery complete once the message is placed on the network. The messages are queued until the receiving applications are ready for them. While the checksum calculation can be used to ensure that the message is correctly received, the messages are not numbered and thus are unsequenced. This type of message delivery is not reliable, but can be used for such activities as trivial file transfer to start up a diskless workstation.

The UDP process must be able to determine the source and destination internet addresses and the protocol field from the internet header which follows the UDP header. Usually, the entire datagram, including the Internet protocol header and the UDP header, is delivered to the application that is using UDP services.

TRANSMISSION CONTROL PROTOCOL (TCP)

Transmission Control Protocol (TCP) provides a highly reliable stream of packets between transport layers on internet hosts by requiring an acknowledgment from the receiving transport layer within a specified period of time and by providing a sequence number to ensure that the packets are delivered in the order that they were sent. Error checking of each packet is provided by a checksum transmitted as part of the TCP header. TCP makes no assumption as to the reliability of the lower-level protocols. To achieve this level of control and reliability, connec-

```
0        4       10          16                          31
```

Source Port							Destination Port	
Sequence Number								
Acknowledgment Number								
Data Offset	Unused	URG	ACK	PSH	RST	SYN	FIN	Window
Checksum							Urgent Pointer	
Options								Padding

FIGURE 18.3   Structure of the Transmission Control Protocol header.

tion from the transport layer on one host to another must be set up before data can be transferred. Figure 18.3 illustrates the information that the transport layer adds when using TCP protocol. TCP's services are used by applications that desire reliable data transmission between hosts. TCP provides a means to recover from lost or damaged data and a means to control the rate at which data is transmitted.

In the TCP header as shown in Figure 18.3, the Source Port field identifies the port number of a source application program while the Destination Port field identifies the port number of the destination application. Thus, many data streams can be set up between the same two hosts using different port numbers. The Checksum field is 16 bits long and is used to verify both the integrity of the segment header and the data. The Data Offset field specifies the offset from the beginning of the message that the data occupies in the message in 32-bit words.

The Sequence Number field specifies the sequence number of this segment of the message and is used to ensure that the segments of a message can be ordered properly and acknowledged individually. The Acknowledgment Number field contains the sequence number of the next segment expected to be received and indicates correct reception of all messages up to that sequence number. Thus, each message can contain both a new message sent to the remote host and the acknowledgment of a received message. As each acknowledgment is received, the segment of the message that it acknowledged is discarded from a *retransmission* queue. If a segment of a message is not acknowledged within a set period of time, that segment is retransmitted.

A set of bits in the middle of the header is used for controlling the connection between the two applications. Each bit has a different function:

- **URG** bit notes that the Urgent pointer is valid.
- **ACK** bit notes that the Acknowledgment field is valid.
- **PSH** bit causes the data in the message to be "pushed" through to the receiving application, even if the buffer is not full.
- **RST** bit resets the connection.
- **SYN** bit resynchronizes the sequence numbers.
- **FIN** bit marks that the sender has reached the end of its byte stream.

Flow control is handled via the Window field which specifies how much data the receiver is willing to accept before another acknowledgment must be received by the sender. The window value is specified when the connection between the applications is established. If one application cannot accept more data from the other, the window field would be set to zero. At the end of the header is room for the variable length options field that is used to indicate the maximum segment size.

ESTABLISHING AND CLOSING CONNECTIONS

A connection between the application on one host and the application of the other host must be established before data can be exchanged between them. A connection is established by the exchanging of several messages as illustrated in Figure 18.4. TCP on Host A initiates the connection by sending a SYN message with an initial sequence number to TCP on Host B (message #1). TCP on Host B acknowledges reception of SYN message from A and transmits its own SYN message with its own initial sequence number (messages #2). TCP on A acknowledges the SYN message of B (message #3) and the connection is established. This is called three-way (or three-message) hand-

TCP on Host A   TCP on Host B

                              (Seq.Num.=100, Code=SYN)
REQUESTING ───► LISTENING

                         (Seq.Num.=300, ACK=101, Code=SYN ACK)
ESTABLISHED ◄─── OK TO CONNECT

                          (Seq.Num.=101, ACK=301, Code=ACK)
ACCEPTED ───► ESTABLISHED

FIGURE 18.4 Establishing a TCP connection between two hosts.

shaking. Initial sequence numbers are chosen based on a fictitious clock that cycles every 4.55 hours. A time-based mechanism is used to avoid reusing sequence numbers too frequently. If a SYN request is received by a TCP process that is not in the ESTABLISHING stage, a reset message must be sent and the connection is closed so that a new connection can be reopened properly synchronized.

A connection is closed by sending a message with the FIN bit set on, indicating no more data to send. No more messages will be sent after that, but messages can still be received and acknowledged in the normal way. After the FIN message has been acknowledged and a FIN message has been received from the other side of the connection, the connect can finally be closed. Figure 18.5 illustrates this sequence of message exchanges. The connection is finally closed after FIN messages have been acknowledged by both sides of the connection.

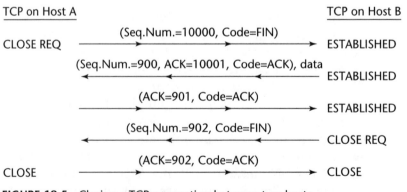

TCP on Host A   TCP on Host B

                              (Seq.Num.=10000, Code=FIN)
CLOSE REQ ──► ESTABLISHED

                    (Seq.Num.=900, ACK=10001, Code=ACK), data
          ◄─── ESTABLISHED

                              (ACK=901, Code=ACK)
          ──► ESTABLISHED

                             (Seq.Num.=902, Code=FIN)
          ◄─── CLOSE REQ

                              (ACK=902, Code=ACK)
CLOSE ──► CLOSE

FIGURE 18.5 Closing a TCP connection between two hosts.

ADDRESSING A PARTICULAR APPLICATION ON A REMOTE HOST

As discussed in Chapter 16, every node must have a unique network address called an internet address. On that node several applications using TCP/IP services can be executing at the same time. How can messages that are destined for one particular application on a particular node be separated from messages destined for another application? The internet layer only passes messages from one node to another node and packages the messages without regard to their application destination. A second level of addressing is used for addressing the particular application of interest; this type of addressing is called *port number addressing*.

When an application starts to use TCP/IP services, it can request an application-based address, a port number. Port numbers are 16 bits long and are assigned by the transport layer. If an application needs to use a particular TCP/IP service, it can do so by addressing that service using a well-known port number which is preassigned. A list of some of these port numbers is in Figure 18.6. These port numbers are registered in a file called /etc/services (discussed in detail in Chapter 8). The well-known services such as **ftp**, **telnet**, and so forth, register their port numbers in this file. For example, **ftp** uses port number 21 for its service requests, while **tftp** uses port number 69. When a user executes a TCP/IP command such as **ftp**, the application will send a message to the well-known port number on the node of interest. The port number of the requesting application will be in the initial message so that the application on the remote host knows the full address of the requesting application. Port numbers are protocol-dependent and the UDP and TCP protocols used in the transport layer can use the same duplicate port numbers because the protocol being used is also in the initial message. Typically, both the same UDP and TCP port numbers are assigned to the well-known services, even though the service may only use one or the other.

Unique port numbers must be used by the applications because another application using that same port number will get messages that are destined for another application. Port

Service Name	Port Number	Description of Service
	0/tcp & 0/udp	Reserved
tcpmux	1/tcp & 1/udp	TCP Port Service Multiplexer
rje	5/tcp & 5/udp	Remote Job Entry
echo	7/tcp & 7/udp	Echo
discard	9/tcp & 9/udp	Discard
systat	11/tcp & 11/udp	Active Users
daytime	13/tcp & 13/udp	Daytime
qotd	17/tcp & 17/udp	Quote of the Day
chargen	19/tcp & 19/udp	Character Generator
ftp-data	20/tcp & 20/udp	File Transfer [Default Data]
ftp	21/tcp & 21/udp	File Transfer [Control]
telnet	23/tcp & 23/udp	Telnet
smtp	25/tcp & 25/udp	Simple Mail Transfer
dsp	33/tcp & 33/udp	Display Support Protocol
time	37/tcp & 37/udp	Time
nameserver	42/tcp & 42/udp	Host Name Server
nicname	43/tcp & 43/udp	Who Is
login	49/tcp & 49/udp	Login Host Protocol
domain	53/tcp & 53/udp	Domain Name Server
bootps	67/tcp & 67/udp	Bootstrap Protocol Server
bootpc	68/tcp & 68/udp	Bootstrap Protocol Client
tftp	69/tcp & 69/udp	Trivial File Transfer
finger	79/tcp & 79/udp	Finger
hostname	101/tcp & 101/udp	NIC Host Name Server
nntp	119/tcp & 119/udp	Network News Transfer Protocol
ntp	123/tcp & 123/udp	Network Time Protocol
exec	512/tcp	Remote process execution; authentication performed using passwords and UNIX login names
biff	512/udp	Used by Mail system to notify users of new mail received

FIGURE 18.6   Some well-known port numbers.

Service Name	Port Number	Description of Service
who	513/udp	Maintains databases showing who is logged in to machines on a local net and the load average of the machine
cmd	514/tcp	Like exec, but automatic authentication is performed as for login server
printer	515/tcp & 515/udp	Spooler
timed	525/tcp & 525/udp	Timeserver
uucp	540/tcp & 540/udp	uucp daemon

FIGURE 18.6 (Continued)

numbers used by applications can be registered in the /etc/services file so that another application does not use it. Once the port number has been registered, other applications that wish to communicate with a particular application can look in the /etc/services file and find out what port number to use. For some services the port number of the requesting application is checked to be sure that it is one of the restricted ones and not one being used by a user application.

A unique connection between two applications can be described by five pieces of information:

    Protocol being used
    Internet address of local node
    Port number of application on local node
    Internet address of remote node
    Port Number of Application on Remote Node

Thus, the full description of an association between two applications would be five pieces of information and can be shown as

```
(TCP, 142.17.3.2, 2145, 142.17.3.3, 21)
```

which might be the description of a connection to ftp on the host with the address 142.17.3.3.

Port numbers less than 1,024 are reserved for specific services. User applications use port numbers that are larger than 1,024 but less than 64,000. In Figure 18.6 some of the port numbers of the well-known services are listed. For example, when a client contacts **ftp** server on a particular host, it uses the well-known port number of the **ftp** server (21) and asks the **tcp** server for a local port number to include in the message so that the **ftp** server can send back responses to the requester of ftp services.

COMPARISON OF SERVICES TCP AND UDP PROVIDE

The transport layer of TCP/IP has two different possible choices: UDP and TCP. An application chooses which of these two protocols to use. Since they offer different services, an application chooses based on which level of service it needs. Figure 18.7 compares the services that these two protocols provide. While TCP offers many more services than UDP does, implementation of an application using TCP will be more complicated. Thus, UDP is suitable for simpler applications like Trivial File Transfer Protocol and booting diskless workstations.

Service	UDP	TCP
Connection-oriented?	N	Y
Message Boundaries?	Y	N
Data Checksum?	Optional	Y
Positive Acknowledgment?	N	Y
Timeout and Retransmit?	N	Y
Duplicate Detection?	N	Y
Sequencing?	N	Y
Flow Control?	N	Y

FIGURE 18.7 Comparison of services UDP and TCP provide.

SUMMARY

This chapter has examined the two protocols that TCP/IP offers in this layer: User Datagram Protocol (UDP) and Transmission Control Protocol (TCP). UDP provides an unreliable, unconnected, datagram-based service while TCP provides a reliable, flow-controlled, connection-based, segment-based service. Both of these services address a particular application on a host using a port number which allows one data stream between the same two hosts to contain messages for several application-to-application communication streams.

UDP is described in great detail in RFC 791, while TCP is similarly described in RFC 793. The table of TCP/IP port assignments is from the RFC entitled "Assigned Numbers" (latest version is RFC 1340) written by J. Reynolds and J. Postel and is available from the RFC source.

Appendix A

TCP/IP Standards Documents

WHAT TCP/IP STANDARDS DOCUMENTS EXIST

The TCP/IP standards are currently being overseen by the Internet Architecture Board (IAB) which is a group of networking users who banded together to organize a worldwide network called the *Internet*. This group is responsible for assigning network addresses and for specifying the protocols that can be used in the Internet. The number of users of the Internet has exploded in the last few years creating an enormous internetwork that is worldwide.

The Internet Architecture Board has chosen to publish its protocol standards in a format called Request for Comments or RFCs. These RFCs cover a variety of topics which may not be intended to be used as standards documents but rather as discussion documents. The number that an RFC has is assigned as soon as it is requested by the author of the soon-to-be-published RFC. RFCs often undergo editing as they are discussed, but as soon as they are formally issued, no further modification of the RFC will occur. In addition, RFC numbers are not reused. But, if new information on a subject needs to be added to an old RFC, the subject can be reused under a new RFC. For example, one particular RFC called "Assigned Numbers" has been issued a number of times as more specifications of TCP/IP values have been added to the RFC. All of this RFC activity can be confusing because a user will want to read the latest RFC on a subject, but how does the user find out which RFC is the latest for that subject?

Two master documents exist which provide an overall guide to the available RFCs and their subjects. The names of the files that these two documents are in are: INDEX.fyi which provides a running commentary on what RFC activities are occurring and INDEX.rfc which lists all the RFCs and their subject and, in particular, indicates which RFC obsoletes which previously issued RFC. These two documents are available from the same sources that the other RFCs are and probably should be read first. The next document to read is the RFC which has IAB Official Protocol Standards as its subject. This document contains a discussion of how the TCP/IP protocol standards process works and the current status of the various standards documents. As an example, this document will list which RFC has the latest list of Assigned Numbers, which RFC describes the File Transfer Protocol, and so forth.

Finally, there are the RFCs themselves. Some of the RFCs are detailed specifications of the various protocols that have been accepted as part of the TCP/IP protocol suite. In addition, there are RFCs that are discussions of various network-related topics and there are even RFCs that are poetry or just commentary on network life.

Figures A.1 through A.4 show the various RFCs that have been written to specify the standards that the Internet Authorization Board has accepted (as of March 1, 1995). For each RFC there is shown both a Status and a State. A shorthand analysis of what the States and Statuses mean is illustrated in Figure A.5. The State of a protocol indicates its maturity. Protocols labelled "std" are part of the set of standard protocols, while the other States indicate the level of discussion and acceptance of a proposed protocol. For example, examining Figure A.1 of Standard Protocols, it can be seen that protocols such as IP and ICMP are required as part of any implementation of TCP/IP protocols, while protocols such as DISCARD or ECHO are optional and can be chosen to be implemented. Protocols such as TCP, UDP, and so on, are in the category where an implementation of TCP/IP should contain them. The Status of a protocol indicates how an implementation of TCP/IP should treat these standards.

Protocol	Name	State	Status	RFC(S)
--------	IAB Official Protocol Standards	Std	Req	1720
--------	Assigned Numbers	Std	Req	1700
--------	Host Requirements—Communications	Std	Req	1122
--------	Host Requirements—Applications	Std	Req	1123
--------	Gateway Requirements	Std	Req	1009
IP	Internet Protocol		Req	791
	as amended by: --------			
--------	IP Subnet Extension	Std	Req	950
--------	IP Broadcast Datagrams	Std	Req	919
--------	IP Broadcast Datagrams w/ Subnets	Std	Req	922
ICMP	Internet Control Message Protocol	Std	Req	792
IGMP	Internet Group Multicast Protocol	Std	Rec	1112
UDP	User Datagram Protocol	Std	Rec	768
TCP	Transmission Control Protocol	Std	Rec	793
TELNET	Telnet Protocol	Std	Rec	854,855
FTP	File Transfer Protocol	Std	Rec	959
SMTP	Simple Mail Transfer Protocol	Std	Rec	821
MAIL	Format of Electronic Mail Messages	Std	Rec	822
CONTENT	Content Type Header Field	Std	Rec	1049
NTP	Network Time Protocol	Std	Rec	1119
DOMAIN	Domain Name System	Std	Rec	1034,1035
DNS-MX	Mail Routing and the Domain System	Std	Rec	974
SNMP	Simple Network Management Protocol	Std	Rec	1157
SMI	Structure of Management Information	Std	Rec	1155
Concise-MIB	Concise MIB Definitions	Std	Rec	1212
MIB-II	Management Information Base-II	Std	Rec	1213
EGP	Exterior Gateway Protocol	Std	Rec	904
NETBIOS	NetBIOS Service Protocols	Std	Ele	1001,1002
ECHO	Echo Protocol	Std	Rec	862
DISCARD	Discard Protocol	Std	Ele	863
CHARGEN	Character Generator Protocol	Std	Ele	864
QUOTE	Quote of the Day Protocol	Std	Ele	865
USERS	Active Users Protocol	Std	Ele	866
DAYTIME	Daytime Protocol	Std	Ele	867
TIME	Time Server Protocol	Std	Ele	868

FIGURE A.1 Standard protocols as specified by the Internet Architecture Board.

Protocol	Name	State	Status	RFC(S)
TFTP	Trivial File Transfer Protocol	Std	Ele	1350
RIP	Routing Information Protocol	Std	Ele	1058
TP-TCP	ISO Transport Service on top of TCP	Std	Ele	1006
ETHER-MIB	Ethernet MIB	Std	Ele	1643
PPP	Point-to-Point Protocol (PPP)	Std	Ele	1661
PPP-HDLC	PPP in HDLC Framing	Std	Ele	1662

FIGURE A.1 (Continued).

Protocol	Name	State	RFC
IP-ATM	Classical IP and ARP over ATM	Prop	1577
IP-FR	Multiprotocol over Frame Relay	Draft	1490
ATM-ENCAP	Multiprotocol Encapsulation over ATM	Prop	1483
IP-TR-MC	IP Multicast over Token-Ring LANs	Prop	1469
IP-FDDI	Transmission of IP and ARP over FDDI Net	Std	1390
IP-HIPPI	IP and ARP on HIPPI	Prop	1374
IP-X.25	X.25 and ISDN in the Packet Mode	Draft	1356
IP-SMDS	IP Datagrams over the SMDS Service	Prop	1209
IP-FDDI	Internet Protocol on FDDI Networks	Draft	1188
ARP	Address Resolution Protocol	Std	826
RARP	A Reverse Address Resolution Protocol	Std	903
IP-ARPA	Internet Protocol on ARPANET	Std	BBN1822
IP-WB	Internet Protocol on Wideband Network	Std	907
IP-E	Internet Protocol on Ethernet Networks	Std	894
IP-EE	Internet Protocol on Exp. Ethernet Nets	Std	895
IP-IEEE	Internet Protocol on IEEE 802	Std	1042
IP-DC	Internet Protocol on DC Networks	Std	891
IP-HC	Internet Protocol on Hyperchannel	Std	1044
IP-ARC	Transmitting IP Traffic over ARCNET Nets	Std	1201
IP-SLIP	Transmission of IP over Serial Lines	Std	1055
IP-NETBIOS	Transmission of IP over NETBIOS	Std	1088
IP-IPX	Transmission of 802.2 over IPX Networks	Std	1132

FIGURE A.2 Network-specific standard protocols as specified by the Internet Architecture Board.

Protocol	Name	State	Status	RFC(S)
FINGER	Finger Protocol	Ele	Draft	1288
BGP3	Border Gateway Protocol 3 (BGP-3)	Ele	Draft	1267,1268
OSPF2	Open Shortest Path First Routing V2	Ele	Draft	1247
POP3	Post Office Protocol, Version 3	Ele	Draft	1225
Concise-MIB	Concise MIB Definitions	Ele	Draft	1212
IP-FDDI	Internet Protocol on FDDI Networks	Ele	Draft	1188
TOPT-LINE	Telnet Linemode Option	Ele	Draft	1184
PPP	Point to Point Protocol	Ele	Draft	1171
BOOTP	Bootstrap Protocol	Rec	Draft	951,1084
TP-TCP	ISO Transport Service on top of TCP	Ele	Draft	1006
NICNAME	WhoIs Protocol	Ele	Draft	954
RIP2-MIB	RIP Version 2 MIB Extension	Ele	Draft	1724
RIP2	RIP Version 2-Carrying Additional Info.	Ele	Draft	1723
RIP2-APP	RIP Version 2 Protocol App. Statement	Ele	Draft	1722
SIP-MIB	SIP Interface Type MIB	Ele	Draft	1694
--------	Def Man Objs Parallel-printer-like	Ele	Draft	1660
--------	Def Man Objs RS-232-like	Ele	Draft	1659
--------	Def Man Objs Character Stream	Ele	Draft	1658
SMTP-SIZE	SMTP Service Ext for Message Size	Ele	Draft	1653
SMTP-8BIT	SMTP Service Ext or 8bit-MIMEtransport	Ele	Draft	1652
SMTP-EXT	SMTP Service Extensions	Ele	Draft	1651
OSI-NSAP	Guidelines for OSI NSAP Allocation	Ele	Draft	1629
ISO-TS-ECHO	Echo for ISO-8473	Ele	Draft	1575
DECNET-MIB	DECNET MIB	Ele	Draft	1559
--------	Message Header Ext. of Non-ASCII Text	Ele	Draft	1522
MIME	Multipurpose Internet Mail Extensions	Ele	Draft	1521
802.3-MIB	IEEE 802.3 Repeater MIB	Ele	Draft	1516
BRIDGE-MIB	BRIDGE-MIB	Ele	Draft	1493
NTPV3	Network Time Protocol (Version 3)	Ele	Draft	1305
IP-MTU	Path MTU Discovery	Ele	Draft	1191

FIGURE A.3 Draft standard protocols as specified by the Internet Architecture Board.

Protocol	Name	State	Status	RFC
TOPT-BIN	Binary Transmission	Std	Rec	856
TOPT-ECHO	Echo	Std	Rec	857
TOPT-RECN	Reconnection	Prop	Ele	. . .
TOPT-SUPP	Suppress Go Ahead	Std	Rec	858
TOPT-APRX	Approx Message Size Negotiation	Prop	Ele	. . .
TOPT-STAT	Status	Std	Rec	859
TOPT-TIM	Timing Mark	Std	Rec	860
TOPT-REM	Remote Controlled Trans and Echo	Prop	Ele	726
TOPT-OLW	Output Line Width	Prop	Ele	. . .
TOPT-OPS	Output Page Size	Prop	Ele	. . .
TOPT-OCRD	Output Carriage-Return Disposition	Prop	Ele	652
TOPT-OHT	Output Horizontal Tabstops	Prop	Ele	653
TOPT-OHTD	Output Horizontal Tab Disposition	Prop	Ele	654
TOPT-OFD	Output Formfeed Disposition	Prop	Ele	655
TOPT-OVT	Output Vertical Tabstops	Prop	Ele	656
TOPT-OVTD	Output Vertical Tab Disposition	Prop	Ele	657
TOPT-OLD	Output Linefeed Disposition	Prop	Ele	658
TOPT-EXT	Extended ASCII	Prop	Ele	698
TOPT-LOGO	Logout	Prop	Ele	727
TOPT-BYTE	Byte Macro	Prop	Ele	735
TOPT-DATA	Data Entry Terminal	Prop	Ele	1043
TOPT-SUP	SUPDUP	Prop	Ele	734
TOPT-SUPO	SUPDUP Output	Prop	Ele	749
TOPT-SNDL	Send Location	Prop	Ele	779
TOPT-TERM	Terminal Type	Prop	Ele	1091
TOPT-EOR	End of Record	Prop	Ele	885
TOPT-TACACS	TACACS User Identification	Prop	Ele	927
TOPT-OM	Output Marking	Prop	Ele	933
TOPT-TLN	Terminal Location Number	Prop	Ele	946
TOPT-3270	Telnet 3270 Regime	Prop	Ele	1041
TOPT-X.3	X.3 PAD	Prop	Ele	1053

FIGURE A.4 Telnet option protocols as specified by the Internet Architecture Board.

Protocol	Name	State	Status	RFC
TOPT-NAWS	Negotiate About Window Size	Prop	Ele	1073
TOPT-TS	Terminal Speed	Prop	Ele	1079
TOPT-RFC	Remote Flow Control	Prop	Ele	1372
TOPT-LINE	Linemode	Draft	Ele	1184
TOPT-XDL	X Display Location	Prop	Ele	1096
TOPT-ENVIR	Telnet Environment Option	Hist	Not	1408
TOPT-AUTH	Telnet Authentication Option	Exp	Ele	1416
TOPT-ENVIR	Telnet Environment Option	Prop	Ele	1572
TOPT-EXTOP	Extended-Options-List	Std	Rec	861

FIGURE A.4 (Continued).

Status	Meaning
Req	Required Protocol; must be implementd
Rec	Recommended Protocol; should be implemented
Ele	Elective Protocol; may be implemented
Lim	Limited Use Protocol; may be implemented
NotRec	Not Recommended Protocol; don't implement

State	Meaning
Std	Standard Protocol
Draft	Draft Standard Protocol; Possible future standard protocol; Being tested; Revision of Draft Standard possible
Prop	Proposed Standard Protocol; Considered for future standard protocol; Being tested by limited groups; Revision of Proposed Standard expected
Exp	Experimental Protocol; Being used for testing purposes only
Info	Informational Protocol; Protocols developed by other organizations and may be recommended for use in the Internet
Hist	Historical Protocol; Unlikely to ever become standard

FIGURE A.5 Various Statuses and States an RFC can have.

HOW TO GET TCP/IP STANDARDS DOCUMENTS

RFCs can be gotten from a number of network sources, but the source for those sources is *nis.nsf.net*. At this location are all of the RFCs, plus many of the discussion documents that are circulated before an RFC is issued. RFCs are available from *nis.nsf.net* via anonymous ftp through the internet. If a user connects to *nis.nsf.net* and then lists the directories that are available, the following will be displayed on the terminal:

```
200 PORT command successful.
 150 Opening ASCII mode data connection for file list.
 lost+found
 netinfo
 bin
 ietf
 dev
 ien
 iso
 scc
 ddn-news
 etc
 home
 protocols
 rfc
 usr
 isode
 tcp-ip
 netinfo:
 std
 internet-drafts
 fyi
 templates
 ddn-news:
 iesg
 domain
 namedroppers
 pub
 demo
 netprog
 226 Transfer complete.
```

If the user changes to the Internet/documents/rfc directory using the **cd internet/documents/rfc** command and executes the **ls** command, a list of all the available RFCs will be displayed in the format rfc*nnnn*.txt where nnnn is the number of the RFC:

```
200 PORT command successful.
 150 Opening ASCII mode data connection for file list.
 rfc-by-author.txt
 rfc-by-title.txt
 rfc-index.txt
 rfc10.txt
 rfc1000.txt
 rfc1001.txt
 rfc1002.txt
 rfc1003.txt
 rfc1004.txt
  (etc.)
```

In addition, two other documents are available (rfc-by-author.txt and rfc-by-title.txt) which list by author or title which RFCs are available. To examine RFC 834, the user would use the **get** command:

```
get rfc834.txt
```

and the rfc 834 would be transferred to the local host.

Many other lists are available from *nis.nsf.net*. For example, if instead of looking for an RFC, the user is looking for a list of the current defined hosts in the internet, the user would change to the domain subdirectory and the following list of files is displayed:

```
150 Opening ASCII mode data connection for /bin/ls.
total 2417
-rw-rw-rw-  1 64         2486 Sep 15 05:13 arpa.zone
-rw-rw-rw-  1 64       870167 Sep 15 19:56 com.zone
-rw-rw-rw-  1 64       205062 Sep 15 20:07 edu.zone
-rw-rw-rw-  1 64        32899 Sep 15 05:18 gov.zone
-rw-rw-rw-  1 64      1027745 Sep 15 05:33 inaddr.zone
-rw-rw-rw-  1 64       145468 Sep 15 20:12 mil.zone
```

```
-rw-rw-rw-  1 64          29884 Sep 15 20:08 net.zone
-rw-rw-rw-  1 64          74834 Sep 15 20:09 org.zone
-rw-rw-rw-  1 64          28853 Sep 15 05:12 root.zone
226 Transfer complete.
```

Thus, for each type of host on the internet, there is a list of currently connected hosts. Each of these lists can be retrieved from the remote host in the usual way.

Appendix B

Glossary of Networking Terms

Many terms are peculiar to networking. This appendix contains acronyms and shorthand ways to refer to various objects that have to do with networking and TCP/IP. Other terms have been added as needed.

ASCII: American Standard Code for Information Interchange. The ASCII character set is as defined in the ARPA-Internet Protocol Handbook. In FTP, ASCII characters are defined to be the lower half of an 8-bit code set (i.e., the most significant bit is zero). In more general terms ASCII is defined by American Standards Institute, X3.4, 1968.

Address Mask: A bit mask used to select bits from an Internet address for subnet addressing. The mask is 32 bits long and selects the network portion of the Internet address and one or more bits of the local portion. Sometimes called subnet mask.

Address Resolution: A means for mapping Network Layer addresses onto media-specific addresses. *See* ARP.

ANSI: American National Standards Institute. The U.S. standardization body. ANSI is a member of the International Organization for Standardization (ISO).

API: Application Program Interface. A set of calling conventions defining how a service is invoked through a software package.

Application Layer: The topmost layer in the TCP/IP Model providing such communication services as electronic mail, file transfer, and remote terminal connection.

ARP: Address Resolution Protocol. The Internet protocol used to dynamically map Internet addresses to physical (hardware) addresses on local area networks. Limited to networks that support hardware broadcast.

ARPA: Advanced Research Projects Agency. Now called DARPA, the U.S. government agency that funded the ARPANET.

ARPANET: A packet-switched network developed in the early 1970s. The "grandfather" of today's Internet. ARPANET was decommissioned in June 1990.

Autonomous System: Internet (TCP/IP) terminology for a collection of gateways (routers) that fall under one administrative entity and cooperate using a common Interior Gateway Protocol (IGP). *See* subnetwork.

Backbone: The primary connectivity mechanism of a hierarchical distributed system. All systems which have connectivity to an intermediate system on the backbone are assured of connectivity to each other. This does not prevent systems from setting up private arrangements with each other to bypass the backbone for reasons of cost, performance, or security.

Baseband: Characteristic of any network technology that uses a single carrier frequency and requires all stations attached to the network to participate in every transmission. *See* broadband.

Bridge: A node connected to two or more administratively indistinguishable but physically distinct subnets, that automatically forwards datagrams when necessary, but whose existence is not known to other hosts. Bridges can usually be made to filter packets, that is, to forward only certain traffic. Also called a software repeater. *See* repeater and router.

Broadband: Characteristic of any network that multiplexes multiple, independent network carriers onto a single cable. This is usually done using frequency division multiplexing. Broadband technology allows several networks to coexist on one single cable; traffic from one network does not interfere with traffic from another since the conversations happen on different frequencies in the "ether", rather like the commercial radio system.

Broadcast: A packet delivery system where a copy of a given packet is given to all hosts attached to the network. Example: Ethernet.

BSD: Berkeley Software Distribution. Term used when describing different versions of the Berkeley UNIX software, as in 4.3BSD UNIX.

Catenet: A network in which hosts are connected to networks with varying characteristics and the networks are interconnected by gateways (routers). The Internet is an example of a catenet.

CCITT: International Consultative Committee for Telegraphy and Telephony. A unit of the International Telecommunications Union (ITU) of the United Nations. An organization with representatives from the PTTs of the world. CCITT produces technical standards, known as Recommendations, for all internationally controlled aspects of analog and digital communications.

Client: A process that requests services from another process, usually called a server. *See* server.

Client-server model: A common way to describe network services and the model user processes (programs) of those services. Examples include the name-server/name-resolver paradigm of the Domain Name System and file-server/file-client relationships such as NFS and diskless hosts. *See* NFS.

Connectionless: The model of interconnection in which communication takes place without first establishing a connection. Sometimes (imprecisely) called datagram. Examples: LANs, Internet IP, UDP, ordinary postcards.

Connection-oriented: The model of interconnection in which communication proceeds through three well-defined phases: connection establishment, data transfer, connection release. Examples: X.25, Internet TCP, ordinary telephone calls.

CSMA/CD: Carrier Sense Multiple Access with Collision Detection. The access method used by local area networking technologies such as Ethernet.

Daemon: Process that runs continuously in the background, waiting for some event to occur or some condition to be true. Daemons are the original method of providing services in a UNIX system. Most servers are daemons.

DARPA: Defense Advanced Research Projects Agency. The U.S. government agency that funded the ARPANET.

Data-Link Layer: The OSI layer that is responsible for data transfer across a single physical connection or series of bridged connections, between two Network entities.

Datagrams: Messages that are sent when no **connection** has been established between two communicating hosts. Each of these messages is treated as an independent unit. UDP protocol sends datagrams.

Destination: The destination address, an internet header field.

DNS: Domain Name System. The distributed name/address mechanism used in the Internet.

Domain: In the Internet, a part of a naming hierarchy. Syntactically, an Internet domain name consists of a series of names (labels) separated by periods (dots), e.g., "tundra.mpk.ca.us."

Dotted decimal notation: The syntactic representation of a 32-bit integer that consists of four 8-bit numbers written in base 10 with periods (dots) separating them. Used to represent IP addresses in the Internet as in: 192.67.67.20.

EGP: Exterior Gateway Protocol. A reachability routing protocol used by gateways in a two-level internet. EGP is used in the Internet core system.

encapsulation: The technique used by layered protocols in which a layer adds header information to the data from the layer above. As an example, in Internet terminology, a packet would contain a header from the physical layer, followed by a header from the network layer (IP), followed by a header from the transport layer (TCP), followed by the application protocol data.

end system: A system which contains application processes capable of communicating through all seven layers of TCP/IP protocols. Equivalent to Internet host.

entity: OSI terminology for a layer protocol machine. An entity within a layer performs the functions of the layer within a single computer system, accessing the layer entity below and providing services to the layer entity above at local service access points.

ethernet: Physical media that is a 10-megabits per second, CSMA/CD baseband network that can be coaxial cable, twisted pairs of wires, or fibre optic cable.

Ethernet Address: Address of a host that is associated with the Ethernet hardware.

File Transfer Protocol (FTP): Protocol that provides file transfer functionality between two dissimilar hosts.

fragmentation: The process in which an IP datagram is broken into smaller pieces to fit the requirements of a given physical network. The reverse process is termed reassembly. *See* MTU.

Frame: A frame is the unit of transmission in a data-link layer protocol and consists of a data-link layer header followed by a packet.

FTP: File Transfer Protocol. The Internet protocol (and program) used to transfer files between hosts.

gateway: A node connected to two or more administratively distinct networks and/or subnets, to which hosts send datagrams to be forwarded. The original Internet term for what is now called router or more precisely, IP router. In modern usage, the terms "gateway" and "application gateway" refer to systems which do translation from some native format to another. Examples include X.400 to/from RFC 822 electronic mail gateways. *See* router.

header: Control information at the beginning of a message, segment, datagram, packet, or block of data.

host: A computer in the internetwork environment on which mailboxes or SMTP processes reside.

IAB: Internet Activities Board. The technical body that oversees the development of the Internet suite of protocols (commonly referred to as TCP/IP). It has two task forces (the IRTF and the IETF), each charged with investigating a particular area.

ICMP: Internet Control Message Protocol. The protocol used to handle errors and control messages at the IP layer. ICMP is used from gateways to hosts and between hosts to report errors and make routing suggestions. ICMP is actually part of the IP protocol.

IESG: Internet Engineering Steering Group. The executive committee of the IETF.

IETF: Internet Engineering Task Force. One of the task forces of the IAB. The IETF is responsible for solving short-term engineering needs of the Internet. It has over 40 Working Groups.

IGP: Interior Gateway Protocol. The protocol used to exchange routing information between collaborating routers in the Internet. RIP and OSPF are examples of IGPs.

intermediate system: A system which is not an end system, but which serves instead to relay communications between end systems. *See* repeater, bridge, and router.

internet: A collection of networks interconnected by a set of routers which allow them to function as a single, large virtual network.

Internet: (note the capital "I") The largest internet in the world consisting of large national backbone nets (such as MILNET, NSFNET, and CREN) and a myriad of regional and local campus networks all over the world. The Internet uses the Internet protocol suite. To be on the Internet you must have IP connectivity, that is, be able to Telnet to—or ping—other systems. Networks with only e-mail connectivity are not actually classified as being on the Internet.

Internet address: A 32-bit address assigned to hosts using TCP/IP. A source or destination address consisting of a Network field and a Local Address field and Possibly a Subnet Number field. *See* dotted decimal notation.

internet datagram: The unit of data exchanged between a pair of internet modules (includes the internet header).

internet fragment: A portion of the data of an internet datagram with an internet header.

IP: Internet Protocol. The network layer protocol for the Internet protocol suite.

IP datagram: The fundamental unit of information passed across the Internet and the unit of end-to-end transmission in IP protocol which contains source and destination addresses along with data and a number of fields which define such things as the length of the datagram, the header checksum, and flags to say whether the datagram can be (or has been) fragmented.

IPng: Internet Protocol next generation. The proposed standard for the internetwork layer for the next century. Features expanded IP address to 128 bits and a definition of authentication and encryption within the internetwork layer.

IRTF: Internet Research Task Force. One of the task forces of the IAB. The group responsible for research and development of the Internet protocol suite.

ISDN: Integrated Services Digital Network. An emerging technology which is beginning to be offered by the telephone carriers of the world. ISDN combines voice and digital network services in a single medium making it possible to offer customers digital data services as well as voice connections through a single "wire." The standards that define ISDN are specified by CCITT.

ISO: International Organization for Standardization is an international standards group which is best known for the seven-layer OSI Reference Model. *See* OSI.

Local Address: The address of a host within a network. The actual mapping of an internet local address on to the host addresses in a network is quite general, allowing for many-to-one mappings.

Local Area Network (LAN): Network of interconnected hosts grouped physically close together, usually in one building or a group of buildings.

mail gateway: A machine that connects two or more electronic mail systems (especially dissimilar mail systems on two different networks) and transfers messages between them. Sometimes the mapping and translation can be quite complex, and generally it requires a store-and-forward scheme whereby the message is received from one system completely before it is transmitted to the next system after suitable translations.

Message: The unit of transmission in a transport layer protocol. In particular, a TCP segment is a message. A message consists of a transport protocol header followed by application protocol data. To be transmitted end-to-end through the Internet, a message must be encapsulated inside a datagram. This term is used by some application layer protocols (particularly SMTP) for an application data unit.

MTU: Maximum Transmission Unit. The largest possible unit of data that can be sent on a given physical medium. Example: The MTU of Ethernet is 1,500 bytes. *See* fragmentation.

multicast: A special form of broadcast where copies of the packet are delivered to only a subset of all possible destinations. *See* broadcast.

multihomed host: A computer connected to more than one physical data link. The data links may or may not be attached to the same network. A host is said to be multihomed if it has multiple IP addresses.

name resolution: The process of mapping a name into the corresponding address. See DNS.

NetBIOS: Network Basic Input Output System. The standard interface to networks on IBM PC and compatible systems.

Network: Collection of processors linked together physically or logically.

Network Layer: The OSI layer that is responsible for routing, switching, and subnetwork access across the entire OSI environment.

NFS(R): Network File System. A distributed file system developed by Sun Microsystems which allows a set of computers to cooperatively access each other's files in a transparent manner.

NIC: Network Information Center. Originally there was only one, located at SRI International and tasked to serve the ARPANET (and later DDN) community. Today, there are many

NICs, by local, regional, and national networks all over the world. Such centers provide user assistance, document service, training, and much more.

node: A computer in the internetwork environment on which internet protocol services are available.

octet: An 8-bit byte.

OSI: Open Systems Interconnection. An international standard-ization program to facilitate communications among computers from different manufacturers. *See* ISO.

OSPF: Open Shortest Path First. A "Proposed Standard" IGP for the Internet. *See* IGP.

Packet: A packet is the unit of data passed across the interface between the internet layer and the link layer. It includes an IP header and data. A packet may be a complete IP datagram or a fragment of an IP datagram.

Path: The sequence of gateways that, at a given moment, all the IP datagrams from a particular source host to a particular desti-nation host will traverse gateways. A path is unidirectional; it is not unusual to have different paths in the two directions between a given host pair.

PDU: Protocol Data Unit. This is OSI terminology for "packet." A PDU is a data object exchanged by protocol machines (enti-ties) within a given layer. PDUs consist of both Protocol Control Information (PCI) and user data.

Physical Layer: The OSI layer that provides the means to acti-vate and use physical connections for bit transmission. In plain terms, the Physical Layer provides the procedures for transfer-ring a single bit across a Physical Media.

Physical Media: Any means in the physical world for transfer-ring signals between OSI systems. Considered to be outside the OSI Model, and therefore sometimes referred to as "Layer 0." The physical connector to the media can be considered as defin-ing the bottom interface of the Physical Layer, i.e., the bottom of the OSI Reference Model.

Physical network interface: This is a physical interface to a connected network and has a (possibly unique) link-layer address. Multiple physical network interfaces on a single host may share the same link-layer address, but the address must be unique for different hosts on the same physical network.

ping: Packet internet groper. A program used to test reachability of destinations by sending them an ICMP echo request and waiting for a reply. The term is used as a verb: "Ping host X to see if it is up !"

port: The entity on a host that performs as a logical network communications channel and is used by Internet transport protocols to distinguish among multiple simultaneous connections to a single destination host. Part of the full address of a particular application on a particular port. A particular port on a host can be addressed by a client to request a particular service. Port numbers are assigned for the standard set of services, called *well-known* ports.

Port Number: Address of an individual application on a particular node. Port numbers less than 1,024 are reserved for standard services.

PPP: Point-to-Point Protocol. The successor to SLIP, PPP provides router-to-router and host-to-network connections over both synchronous and asynchronous circuits. *See* SLIP.

Presentation Layer: The OSI layer that determines how Application information is represented (i.e., encoded) while in transit between two end systems.

protocol: A formal description of messages to be exchanged and rules to be followed for two or more systems to exchange information.

proxy: The mechanism whereby one system "fronts for" another system in responding to protocol requests. Proxy systems are used in network management to avoid having to implement full protocol stacks in simple devices, such as modems.

proxy ARP: The technique in which one machine, usually a router, answers ARP requests intended for another machine. By "faking" its identity, the router accepts responsibility for routing packets to the "real" destination. Proxy ARP allows a site to use a single IP address with two physical networks. Subnetting would normally be a better solution.

RARP: Reverse Address Resolution Protocol. The Internet protocol a diskless host uses to find its Internet address at startup. RARP maps a physical (hardware) address to an Internet address. *See* ARP.

repeater: A device which propagates electrical signals from one cable to another without making routing decisions or providing packet filtering. In OSI terminology, a repeater is a Physical Layer intermediate system. *See* bridge and router.

RFC: Request For Comments. The document series, begun in 1969, which describes the Internet suite of protocols and related experiments. Not all (in fact very few) RFCs describe Internet standards, but all Internet standards are written up as RFCs.

RFS: Remote File System. A distributed file system, similar to NFS, developed by AT&T and distributed with their UNIX System V operating system. *See* NFS.

RIP: Routing Information Protocol. An Interior Gateway Protocol (IGP) supplied with Berkeley UNIX.

rlogin: A service offered by Berkeley UNIX which allows users of one machine to log into other UNIX systems (for which they are authorized) and interact as if their terminals were connected directly. Similar to Telnet.

router: A system responsible for making decisions about which of several paths network or internetwork traffic will follow. To do this it uses a routing protocol to gain information about the network, and a set of algorithms to choose the best route based on several criteria known as "routing metrics." In OSI terminology, a router is a Network Layer intermediate system. *See* gateway, bridge and repeater.

RPC: Remote Procedure Call. An easy and popular paradigm for implementing the client-server model of distributed computing. A request is sent to a remote system to execute a designated procedure, using arguments supplied, and the result returned to the caller. There are many variations and subtleties, resulting in a variety of different RPC protocols.

Segment: A segment is the unit of end-to-end transmission in the TCP protocol. A segment consists of a TCP header followed by application data. A segment is transmitted by encapsulation inside an IP datagram.

Server: The entity that provides services when it is requested by a client. Servers are usually daemons on a UNIX system. *See* client-server model, daemon.

Session: The set of transactions that are exchanged while the transmission channel is open.

Session Layer: The OSI layer that provides the pathway for dialogue control between end systems.

SLIP: Serial Line Internet Protocol. An Internet protocol used to run IP over serial lines such as telephone circuits or RS-232 cables interconnecting two systems. SLIP is now being replaced by PPP. *See* PPP.

SMI: Structure of Management Information. The rules used to define the objects that can be accessed via a network management protocol.

SMTP: Simple Mail Transfer Protocol. The Internet electronic mail protocol. Defined in RFC 821, with associated message format descriptions in RFC 822.

SNMP: Simple Network Management Protocol. The network management protocol of choice for TCP/IP-based internets.

Source: The source address, an internet header field.

Subnet: A single member of the collection of hardware networks that compose an IP network. Host addresses on a given subnet share an IP network number with hosts on all other subnets of that IP network, but the local-address part is divided into subnet-number and host-number fields to indicate which subnet a host is on. A particular division of the local-address part is not assumed; this could vary from network to network.

Subnet Field: The bit field in an Internet address denoting the subnet number. The bits making up this field are not necessarily contiguous in the address.

subnet mask: The designation of which bits in the internet dotted decimal scheme of addresses form the subnet number. *See* address mask.

subnetwork: A collection of end systems and intermediate systems under the control of a single administrative domain and utilizing a single network access protocol. Examples: private X.25 networks, collection of bridged LANs.

Subnet Number: A number identifying a subnet within a network.

TCP: Transmission Control Protocol. The major transport protocol in the Internet suite of protocols providing reliable, connection-oriented, full-duplex streams. Uses IP for delivery.

TCP Segment: The unit of data exchanged between TCP modules (including the TCP header).

Telnet: The virtual terminal protocol in the Internet suite of protocols. Allows users of one host to log into a remote host and interact as normal terminal users of that host.

TFTP: Trivial File Transfer Protocol: A simple file transfer protocol built on UDP.

transaction: The set of exchanges required for one message to be transmitted for one or more recipients.

transceiver: Transmitter-receiver. The physical device that connects a host interface to a local area network, such as Ethernet. Ethernet transceivers contain electronics that apply signals to the cable and sense collisions.

transmission channel: A full-duplex communication path between a sender-SMTP and a receiver-SMTP for the exchange of commands, replies, and mail text.

Transport Layer: The OSI layer that is responsible for reliable end-to-end data transfer between end systems.

transport service: Any reliable stream-oriented data communication services. For example, TCP.

Virtual Circuit: Connection that is established between two application programs (for example, a **telnet** connection). To establish a connection requires a specific sequence of operations. The establishment of a circuit is most effective in the case where a number of messages are going to be exchanged.

UDP: User Datagram Protocol. A transport protocol in the Internet suite of protocols. UDP, like TCP, uses IP for delivery; however, unlike TCP, UDP provides for exchange of datagrams without acknowledgments or guaranteed delivery.

UDP Datagram: A UDP datagram is the unit of end-to-end transmission in the UDP protocol.

UUCP: UNIX to UNIX Copy Program. A protocol used for communication between consenting UNIX systems.

Wide Area Network (WAN): Network of communicating hosts that are connected together using telephone line services, geographically spread out over a wide area.

XDR: eXternal Data Representation. A standard for machine-independent data structures developed by Sun Microsystems. Similar to ASN.1.

SUMMARY

Many of the RFCs that have been published by the IAB have extensive sections on terminology. In addition, RFC1240 contains just terminology and acronyms used in the RFC literature. The various RFCs provide the basis for an extensive glossary of terms and acronyms.

Index